25th DEC 1986.

2 MUM
Happy christmas
Happy new year
Lots of love
TiNA x x x
x x
x.

Microwave
COOKING FOR 1&2

BRAMLEY BOOKS

Compiled and Edited by Judith Ferguson
Designed by Philip Clucas
Photography by Peter Barry
Produced by Ted Smart,
David Gibbon and Gerald Hughes

CLB 1742
This edition published 1986 by Bramley Books, Godalming, Surrey.
© 1986 Illustrations and text: Colour Library Books Ltd.,
    Guildford, Surrey.
Printed and bound in Barcelona, Spain.
ISBN 0 86283 493 7

CONTENTS

GENERAL INTRODUCTION

People are usually of two minds about microwave ovens. Experienced cooks are sceptical. Inexperienced cooks are mystified. Most people who don't own one think a microwave oven is an expensive luxury. Those of us who have one, though, would find it difficult to give it up. Great advances have been made in the design and capabilities of microwave ovens since the demand for them first began in the Sixties. With so many kinds of ovens available, both beginners and advanced cooks can find one that best suits their particular needs.

How Microwave Ovens Work

Microwave ovens, whatever the make or model, do have certain things in common. The energy that makes fast cooking possible is comprised of electromagnetic waves converted from electricity. Microwaves are a type of high frequency radio wave. The waves are of short length, hence the name microwave.

Inside the oven is a magnetron, which converts ordinary electricity into microwaves. A wave guide channels the microwaves into the oven cavity, and a stirrer fan circulates them evenly. Microwaves are attracted to the particles of moisture that form part of any food. As the microwaves are absorbed, to a depth of about 4-5cm/$1^{1}/_{2}$-2 inches, they cause the water molecules in the food to vibrate, about 2000 million times a second. This generates the heat that cooks the food. The heat reaches the centre of the food by conduction, just as in ordinary cooking. However, this is accomplished much faster than in conventional cooking because no heat is generated until the waves are absorbed by the food. All the energy is concentrated on cooking the food and not on heating the oven itself or the baking dishes. Standing time is often necessary to allow the food to continue cooking after it is removed from the oven.

Most microwave ovens have an ON indicator light and a timer control. Some timer controls look like minute timers, while others are calibrated in seconds up to 50 seconds and minutes up to 30 minutes. This can vary slightly; some models have a 10 minute interval setting. Some ovens have a separate ON-OFF switch, while others switch on with the timer or power setting. Almost all have a bell or buzzer to signal the end of cooking time.

Microwave Oven Features

At this point, things really begin to diversify. Different terms are used for the same power setting depending on what brand of oven you buy. Some ovens have a wider range of different settings as well. Chart No. 1 on power settings reconciles most of the popular terms.

Some ovens come equipped with a temperature probe which allows you to cook food according to its internal temperature instead of by time. It is most useful for roasting large cuts of meat. The probe needle is inserted into the thickest part of the food and the correct temperature set on the attached control. When that internal temperature is reached, the oven automatically turns off, or switches to a low setting to keep the food warm. Special microwave thermometers are also available to test internal temperature and can be used inside the oven. Conventional thermometers must never be used inside a microwave oven, but can be used outside.

A cooking guide is a feature on some ovens, either integrated into the control panel or on the top or side of the oven housing. It is really a summary of the information found in the instruction and recipe booklet that accompanies every oven. However, it does act as a quick reference and so can be a time saver.

CHART 1 Power Setting Comparison Chart

	Other Terms and Wattages	Uses
Low	ONE or TWO, KEEP WARM, 25%, SIMMER, DEFROST. 75-300 watts.	Keeping food warm. Softening butter, cream cheese and chocolate. Heating liquid to dissolve yeast. Gentle cooking.
Medium	THREE or FOUR, 50%, STEW, BRAISE, ROAST, REHEAT, MEDIUM-LOW, FIVE, 40%, MEDIUM-HIGH, SIX, 60-75%.. 400-500 watts.	Roasting meat and poultry. Stewing and braising less tender cuts of meat. Baking cakes and custards. Cooking hollandaise sauces.
High	SEVEN, FULL, ROAST, BAKE, NORMAL, 100%.	Quick cooking. Meats, fish, vegetables, biscuits/cookies, pasta, rice, breads, pastry, desserts.

Turntables eliminate the need for rotating baking dishes during cooking, although when using a square or loaf dish you may need to change its position from time to time anyway. Turntables are usually glass or ceramic and can be removed for easy cleaning. Of all the special features available, turntables are one of the most useful.

Certain ovens have one or more shelves so that several dishes can be accommodated at once. Microwave energy is higher at the top of the oven than on the floor and the more you cook at once the longer it all takes. However, these ovens accommodate larger baking dishes than those with turntables.

If you do a lot of entertaining, then an oven with a keep warm setting is a good choice. These ovens have a very low power setting that can keep food warm without further cooking for up to one hour. If you want to programme your oven like a computer, choose one with a memory control that can switch settings automatically during the cooking cycle.

Browning elements are now available built into microwave ovens. They look and operate much the same as conventional electric grills. If you already have a grill, you probably don't need a browning element. Some of the most recent ovens allow the browning element to be used at the same time as the microwave setting, which is a plus.

Combination ovens seem to be the answer to the problem of browning in a microwave oven. While the power settings go by different names in different models, generally there is a setting for microwave cooking alone, a convection setting with conventional electric heat and a setting which combines the two for almost the speed of microwave cooking with the browning ability of convection heat. However, the wattage is usually lower than in standard microwave ovens, and so cooking time will be slightly longer.

On combination settings, use recipes developed for microwave ovens, but follow the instructions with your particular oven for times and settings. Some ovens have various temperature settings to choose from. Breads, poultry, meat and pastries brown beautifully in these ovens, and conventional baking dishes, even metal, can be used with a special insulating mat. Beware of certain plastics though, as they can melt in a combination oven.

You can have your microwave oven built into the same unit as your conventional oven. Microwave ovens are best situated at eye level. In fact, there are now units available with gas or electric cooktops and a microwave oven underneath where the conventional oven used to be.

Safety and Cleaning

One of the questions most commonly asked is "Are microwave ovens safe to use?" They are safe because they have safety features built into them and they go through rigorous tests by their manufacturers and by independent agencies.

If you look at a number of microwave ovens you will see that the majority of them are lined with metal, and metal will not allow microwaves to pass through. The doors have special seals to keep the microwaves inside the oven and have cut-out devices to cut off microwave energy immediately the door is opened. There are no pans to upset, no open flames or hot elements and the interior of the oven stays cool enough to touch. Although microwave ovens don't heat baking dishes, the heat generated by the cooking food does, so it is a good idea to use oven gloves or pot holders to remove dishes from the oven. It is wise periodically to check the door of your oven to make sure it has not been bent. Check latches and hinges, too, to make sure they are in good working order. Don't use baking dishes that are too large to allow the turntable to rotate freely; this can cause the motor to over-heat or cause dents in the oven sides and door, lowering efficiency and affecting safety of operation.

Microwave ovens are cleaner and more hygienic to cook with than conventional gas and electric ovens. Foods do not spatter as much and spills do not burn, so clean-up is faster. The turntables and shelves can be removed for easier cleaning. Use non-abrasive cleansers and scrubbers, and be sure to wipe up

A special microwave thermometer, which is used to test the internal temperature of the food, can be used inside the oven.

any residue so that it does not build up around the door seals. Faster cooking times and lower electricity consumption combine to make microwave ovens cheaper to run, especially for cooking small amounts of food, than conventional ovens.

Once you have chosen your oven and understand what makes it work, the fun of cooking begins. There are some basic rules to remember, however, as with conventional cooking, but most of them are common sense.

Quantity

Food quantities affect cooking times. For example, one baked potato will take about 3-4 minutes, two will take about 6-7 minutes, four will take 10-11 minutes. Generally, if you double the quantity of a recipe, you need to increase the cooking time by about half as much again.

Density and Shape

The denser the food, the longer the cooking time. A large piece of meat is bound to take longer to cook than something light and porous like a cake or a loaf of bread. When cooking foods of various densities or shapes at the same time, special arrangements are necessary. For instance, place the thicker part of the food to the outside of the dish, thinner part toward the middle. Arrange pieces of food in a circle whenever possible, and in a round dish. If neither of these arrangements is possible, cover the thinner or less dense part of the food with foil for part of the cooking time. Rearrange and turn over such foods as asparagus or broccoli spears several times during cooking if they will not fit into your round dishes without considerable trimming.

Size

The smaller a piece of food the quicker it will cook. Pieces of food of the same kind and size will cook at the same rate. Add smaller or faster-cooking foods further along in the cooking time, such as mushrooms to a stew. If you have a choice of cooking heights, put food that is larger and can take more heat above food that is smaller and more delicate.

Covering

Most foods will cook, reheat or defrost better when covered. Use special covers that come with your cookware or simple cover with cling film. This covering must be pierced to release steam, otherwise it can balloon and possibly burst. Tight covering can give meat and poultry a "steamed" taste. Greaseproof paper or paper towels can also be used to keep in the heat and increase cooking efficiency.

Sugar or Fat Content

High sugar or fat content in certain foods means they will absorb microwave energy faster and reach a higher temperature. It is wise to cover food that will spatter, such as bacon, and to protect cakes that have very sugary toppings.

Standing Time

Microwave recipes usually advise leaving food to stand for 5-10 minutes after removal from the oven. Slightly undercooking the food allows the residual heat to finish it off, and microwave recipes take this into consideration. Meat and baked potatoes are usually wrapped in foil to contain the heat. Standing time also makes meat easier to carve. Cakes, breads and pastries should be left on a flat surface for their standing time as this helps to cook their bases. In general, foods benefit from being covered during standing time.

Equipment and Cookware

The number of different baking dishes and the range of equipment for microwave cooking is vast. There are so many highly specialised dishes for specific needs that to list them all would take up almost the whole of this book!

Explore cookware departments and find your own favourites. Follow your oven instruction booklet carefully since it will give you good advice on which cookware is best for your particular oven. Some dishes, lightweight plastics and even some hard plastics can't be used on combination settings. The temperature is too high and the dishes will melt or break. Most metal cookware can be used successfully in combination ovens, following the manufacturers guidelines. I have had less than satisfactory results with certain aluminium pans in my combination oven, so experimentation is essential. Paper bags can catch fire on High settings, and I have had the same experience with silicone-coated paper, although its use is often recommended. Microwave energy penetrates round shapes particularly efficiently, so round dishes and ring moulds work very well. The turntable can also be cooked on directly for such foods as scones or meringues or used for reheating foods like bread or coffee cakes.

Above and left: the number and variety of different baking dishes and the range of equipment for the microwave is vast.

For foods that are likely to boil over, like jams and soups, use the largest, deepest bowl that will fit into the oven cavity. Whole fish can be cooked in a cooking bag and curved to fit the shape of the turntable if they are too large to lie flat.

Browning dishes do work and the results are impressive. There are different designs and some have lids so that meat can be browned and finished off as a braise or stew in the same dish. Covering foods like chops or nut cutlets also speeds up the browning process. These dishes need to be preheated for between 4 to 8 minutes, depending on manufacturers instructions, and will get extremely hot. Use oven gloves or pot holders to remove browning dishes from the oven and set them on a heatproof mat to protect work surfaces. Butter will brown very fast, and steaks and chops can be seared. Stir frying is possible in a microwave oven with the use of a browning tray, and sausages brown beautifully without the shrinkage of conventional grilling or frying. These dishes can also be useful for browning a flour and fat roux for making sauces and gravies.

Cooking Poultry, Meat and Game

Moisture evaporates less readily during microwave cooking, so meat does not dry out. The fat in poultry will turn brown during cooking, but only in whole birds. Single joints of chicken or other poultry cook too quickly for the fat to brown. A thin layer of fat left on pork or beef for roasting will also brown, although it will not crisp. Fat is important to help keep the meat moist, but if you prefer to take it off, do so after cooking, or remember to baste frequently and cover the meat. There are a number of bastes, coatings and seasonings, some especially developed for microwave cooking, that can be used to give an appetizing brownness to meat and poultry.

Choose boned and rolled joints and cuts of meat that are a uniform thickness and shape. If this isn't possible, the next best thing is covering the thinner parts with foil for part of the cooking time. This trick with foil is also useful on poultry to cover the leg ends and the meat along the length of the breast bone. For poultry joints, cover the thinner ends of the breasts and the drumsticks.

Less tender cuts of meat, such as those for stewing, need to be cooked on a medium setting after initial browning. High settings can toughen these cuts of meat. Whether or not to salt meat before cooking depends on which book you read. I think the general rules that apply to conventional meat cooking apply to microwave cooking as well. Do not salt meat to be roasted until after cooking. Sprinkle salt inside the cavity of poultry, if desired, and lightly salt stews and braises once the liquid has been added. Charts No. 2 and 3 serve as a quick reference, for meat, poultry and game.

Cooking Fish and Shellfish

The microwave oven excels at cooking fish. You can poach fish fillets in minutes. Arrange them in a dish in a circle with the thicker part of the fillet to the outside of the dish. If preparing a sauce to go with the fish, poach in a little white wine or water and lemon juice for a little more liquid to work with. A bay leaf, slice of onion and a few peppercorns are classic additions to the poaching liquid for extra flavour.

CHART 2 Meat, Poultry and Game (per 450g/1lb.)

	Mins. on High	Mins. on Medium	Internal Temperature Before Standing	After Standing
Beef: boned and rolled				
rare	6-7	11-13	57°C/130°F	62°C/140°F
medium	7-8	13-15	65°C/150°F	70°C/160°F
well-done	8-9	15-17	70°C/160°F	78°C/170°F
Beef: bone in				
rare	5	10	57°C/130°F	62°C/140°F
medium	6	11	65°C/150°F	70°C/160°F
well-done	8	15	70°C/160°F	78°C/170°F
Leg of Lamb	8-10	11-13	78°C/170°F	82°C/180°F
Veal	8-9	11-12	70°C/160°F	78°C/170°F
Pork	9-11	13-15	82°C/180°F	85°C/185°F
Ham				
Uncooked, boned	1st 5	15-18	55°C/130°F	70°C/160°F
Bone in	1st 5	15½-18½	55°C/130°F	70°C/160°F
Pre-cooked, boned	1st 5	12-15	55°C/130°F	
Bone in	1st 5	10-15		
Chicken	6-8	9-11	85°C/185°F	94°C/190°F
Duck	6-8	9-11	85°C/185°F	94°C/190°F
Turkey	9-11	12-15	85°C/185°F	94°C/190°F
Pheasant		20 total		
Poussins	15-20 total			
Wild Duck	5	10 total		
Pigeon	10 total			
Quail	5-9 total			

CHART 3 Small Cuts of Meat, Poultry and Game

Type	Mins. on High	Mins. on Medium	Special Instructions
Steaks (3.75mm/ 1½″ thick) 120g-180g/4-6oz			Use a browning dish pre-heated to manufacturer's instructions. Use timing for rare when cooking kebabs.
rare	2-3		
medium rare	3-4		
medium	5-7		
well-done	7-9		
Lamb Chops	7-9	13-15	Use a browning dish Cook in liquid
Lamb Fillet		10-12	Brown, then cook in liquid
Pork Chops	7-9	13-15	Use a browning dish Cook in liquid
Pork Fillet		15	Brown, then cook in liquid
Veal Chops	7-9	13-15	Use a browning dish Cook in liquid
Smoked Pork Chops	4-6		Pre-cooked and browned
Ham Steaks	3		Pre-cooked and browned
Minced/Ground Meat (450g/1lb)	5		Break up with a fork as it cooks
Hamburgers	2½-3		Use browning dish
Lamb Patties	2½-3		Use browning dish
Meatballs (675g/1½ lbs)	10-12		
Duck Portions			Use browning dish
1 Breast (boned)	6		
2 Legs		15	Brown each side first
Chicken			
1 Breast		2-3	Brown first if desired
1 Leg		3-4	
2 Pieces		3-6	
3 Pieces		4-7	
4 Pieces		7-9	
Turkey Escalopes/Cutlets		10-15	
Turkey Legs (450g/1lb)	1st 10	13-16	
Bacon	4 1		On rack or paper towels Per side on pre-heated browning dish
Sausages	2		Use browning dish

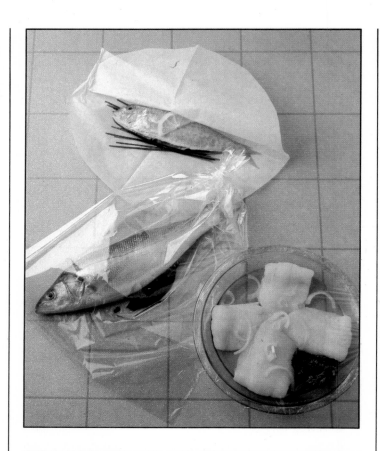

CHART 4 Fish and Shellfish (per 450g/1lb.)

Type	Mins. on high	Type	Mins. on high
Cod Steaks and Fillets	4-5	Salmon (Whole, 1kg/2.2lbs)	10-15
Halibut and Turbot Steaks and Fillets	4-5	Salmon Steaks and Tail pieces	2-7
Smoked Fish (poached)	1-2	Sea Bass (Whole, 1kg/2.2lbs)	10-15
Sole Fillets	2-3	Prawns/Shrimp Scampi/Langoustines	2-5
Mackerel	10-12	Scallops	2-5
Trout	8-10	Mussels	2-3
Herring Fillets	6-8	Oysters	1-2
Tuna Steaks	5	Squid	6
Monkfish Tail Portion Sliced	8-9 2-5		

Whole fish can be "fried" in a browning dish. They can also be cooked in bags, shallow covered dishes or enclosed in greaseproof paper — en papillote.

Shellfish can toughen if cooked too quickly at too high a temperature. Add them to a hot sauce and leave for 5 minutes to cook in residual heat. Alternatively, cook on their own for no more than 3 minutes.

See chart No. 4 for times and settings.

Cooking Vegetables

Microwave cooking is ideal for vegetables. Very little water is needed, so they keep their colour and nutrients. They are best cooked loosely covered, and whole vegetables like corn-on-the-cob, aubergines, artichokes and chicory can be completely wrapped in cling film and cooked without any water. Cooking bags are another alternative.

   Break broccoli into even-sized pieces and, if cooking a large quantity, be sure to put the flower ends in toward the centre of the dish. Trim down the tough ends of asparagus and peel the ends of the stalks. This will help the stalks cook quickly before the tips are overcooked. Some vegetables, like cucumbers, spring onions and button onions cook very well in butter or margarine alone, if well covered. Chart No. 5 lists suggested cooking times.

Cooking Fruit

Poach, bake and preserve fruit with ease in a microwave oven. Sterilise jars for preserving by adding a little water and heating on High for about 2-3 minutes and then draining. Metal lids and rubbers seals are best sterilised outside the microwave oven.

CHART 5 Cooking Vegetables

Type	Quantity	Water	Mins. on High	Mins. Stdg. Time
Artichokes	4	430ml/¾pt/1½ cups	10-20	5
Asparagus	450g/1lb	140ml/¼pt/½ cup	9-12	5
Aubergine/Eggplant	2 med.	30ml/2 tbsps	7-10	5
Beans	450g/1lb	140ml/¼pt/½ cup		
Green, French			8	3
Broad/Lima			10	3
Beetroot/Beets Whole	2	60ml/2 fl oz/¼ cup	4-5	3
Broccoli	450g/1lb	140ml/¼ pt/½ cup	4-5	3
Brussels Sprouts	450g/1lb	60ml/2 fl oz/¼ cup	8-10	3-5
Cabbage	450g/1lb	140ml/¼ pint/½ cup		
Shredded			7-9	3
Quartered			9-12	5
Carrots	225g/8oz	140ml/¼ pint/½ cup		
Whole			10	6
Sliced			7	5
Cauliflower	450g/1lb			
Whole		280ml/½ pint/1 cup	11	3
Florets		140ml/¼ pint/½ cup	7	3
Chicory	4	60ml/2 fl oz/¼ cup (water or stock)	5	3
Corn-on-the-Cob	2 ears	60ml/2 fl oz/¼ cup	6	3
Courgettes/Zucchini	450g/1lb	60ml/2 fl oz/¼ cup	5	3
Fennel	1 bulb	280ml/½ pint/1 cup boiling water		
Sliced			2-8	3
Quartered			10-12	3
Leeks, sliced	450g/1lb	140ml/¼ pint/½ cup	7-10	3
Mushrooms	225g/8oz	30ml/2 tbsps	2	3
Okra	225g/8oz	60ml/2 fl oz/¼ cup	4	3
Onions, small	225g/8oz	30ml/1 fl oz/2 tbsps	7-8	3
Sliced	2	60ml/2 fl oz/¼ cup	10	3
Parsnips	225g/8oz	140ml/¼ pint/½ cup	8-10	3
Peas, shelled	450g/1lb	140ml/¼ pint/½ cup	10-15	5
Peapods/Mangetout	225g/8oz	140ml/¼ pint/½ cup	3	3
Peppers	2 sliced	60ml/2 fl oz/¼ cup	3	3
Potatoes				
New	450g/1lb	140ml/¼ pint/½ cup	10-12	5
Baked	2		9-12	10
Boiled	450g/1lb	140ml/¼ pint/½ cup	6-7	5
Spinach	225g/8oz		4-5	3
Turnips	225g/8oz	60ml/2 fl oz/¼ cup	12	3

Paraffin wax for sealing jars cannot be melted in a microwave oven. The great advantages of microwave preserving are that jams and jellies can be made in small amounts and the job is much less messy and time-consuming. Whole preserved fruits and pickled vegetables can't be heated long enough to kill bacteria, so they must be kept refrigerated after bottling.

Cooking Rice, Pasta, Grains and Pulses

Rice and pasta need nearly as much cooking by microwave methods as by conventional ones. However, both pasta and rice cook without sticking together and without the chance of overcooking. This is because most of the actual cooking is accomplished during standing time. All kinds of rice and shapes of pasta benefit from being put into hot water with a pinch of salt and 5ml/l tsp oil in a deep bowl. There is no need to cover the bowl during cooking, but, during standing time, a covering of some sort will help retain heat. Ease long spaghetti into the bowl gradually as it softens. Drain rice and pasta and rinse under hot water to remove starch. Both pasta and rice can be reheated in a microwave oven without loss of texture. Fresh pasta doesn't seem to take to the microwave oven successfully.

There is a great time saving with dried peas, beans and lentils — pulses. Cover them with water in a large bowl and heat on a High setting to bring to the boil, which takes about 10 minutes. Allow the pulses to boil for about 2 minutes and then leave to stand for one hour. This cuts out overnight soaking. The pulses will cook in about 45 minutes to one hour depending on what variety is used. This is about half the conventional cooking time. Make sure pulses are cooked completely; it can be dangerous to eat them undercooked. Refer to Chart No. 6 for cooking times.

Cooking Eggs and Cheese

When poaching eggs, always pierce the yolks with a skewer or fork to prevent them from bursting. Use individual ramekins or patty pans with a spoonful of water in each. Alternatively, bring water to the boil in a large dish and add a pinch of salt and 5ml/l tsp vinegar to help set the egg whites. Slip the eggs in one at a time. Cook just until the whites are set. To stop the cooking and to keep the eggs from drying out, keep them in a bowl of cold water. For frying eggs, choose a browning dish, and for

Microwave ovens can cut the rising time for yeast doughs nearly in half, and a loaf of bread will bake in an astonishing 8-10 minutes.

Biscuits will not usually crisp in a microwave oven except in one with a combination setting. However, they bake to a moist, chewy texture which is just as pleasing. A batch of 3 dozen will cook in about 10 minutes.

Pastry is not as much of a problem as most people believe. Prick the base and sides of the pastry well, after lining a pie or flan dish. It is essential to bake the pastry shell "blind" — without filling — in order to dry the base. Pastry will not bake to an even brown. The exception is, of course, pastry baked in a combination oven. Pastry and filling can be baked at the same time in these ovens.

CHART 6 Cooking Rice, Pasta, Grains and Pulses

Type	Quantity	Water	Mins. on High	Mins. Stdg. Time
Brown Rice	120g/4oz/ 1 cup	570ml/1 pint/ 2 cups	20	5
White Rice (long grain)	120g/4oz/ 1 cup	570ml/1 pint/ 2 cups	10-12	5
Quick Cooking Rice	120g/4oz/ 1 cup	430ml/¾ pint/ 1½ cups	6	5
Macaroni	225g/8oz/ 3 cups	1 litre/1¾ pints/ 3½ cups	6	10
Quick Cooking Macaroni	225g/8oz/ 3 cups	1 litre/1¾ pints/ 3½ cups	3	10
Spaghetti	225g/8oz	1 litre/1¾ pints/ 3½ cups	6-10	10
Tagliatelle/Fettucine	225g/8oz	1 litre/1¾ pints/ 3½ cups	5-9	10
Pasta Shapes	225g/8oz/ 3 cups	1 litre/1¾ pints/ 3½ cups	6	10
Lasagne Ravioli Cannelloni	180g-225g/ 6oz-8oz	1 litre/1¾ pints/ 3½ cups	6	10
Barley	120g/4oz/ 1 cup	570ml/1 pint/ 2 cups	20	10
Bulgur (cracked wheat)	225g/8oz/ 2 cups	570ml/1 pint/ 2 cups boiling water	4	10
Dried Beans	180g/6oz/ 1 cup	1 litre/1¾ pints/ 3½ cups	55-60	10
Dried Peas	225g/8oz/ 3 cups	1 litre/1¾ pints/ 3½ cups	45-60	10
Lentils	225g/8oz/ 3 cups	1 litre/1¾ pints/ 3½ cups	20-25	15

NOTE: Add a pinch of salt and 5ml/1 tsp oil to grains and pasta

scrambling use a deep bowl or glass measuring jug. Always remove scrambled eggs from the oven while they are still very soft. Stir during standing time to finish cooking. Hollandaise sauce is easy to make. Choose the same kind of container as for scrambled eggs and have a bowl of iced water ready. Use a medium setting and cook the sauce at short intervals, whisking vigorously in between times. Put the sauce bowl into the iced water at the first sign of curdling or briefly when it has thickened, to stop the cooking process.

Cheese will get very stringy if it overcooks or gets too hot. When preparing a cheese sauce, stir finely grated cheese into the hot sauce base and leave to stand. The cheese will melt without further cooking. Cheese toppings will not brown except in a combination oven. A medium setting is best for cheese.

Baking

Baking is one of the most surprising things a microwave oven does. Quick breads, those leavened with baking powder or soda and sour milk, rise higher than they do in a conventional oven and bake faster. If using a square or loaf dish, cover the corners with foil for part of the cooking time to keep that part of the bread or cake from drying out before the middle is cooked. Cakes also rise much higher and a single layer will bake in about 6 minutes on a medium setting.

CHART 7 Reheating

	Quantity	Setting	Time from room temp. (minutes)	Special Instructions
Spaghetti Sauce	225g/8oz 450g/1lb	Med.	5-6 7-8	Stir several times. Keep loosely covered.
Beef Stew	225g/8oz 450g/1lb	Med.	5-5½ 6-7	Stir occasionally. Cover loosely.
Casseroles	225g/8oz 450g/1lb	Med.	5-7 7-8	Stir occasionally. Cover loosely. Use the shorter time for chicken, fish or vegetables.
Chili	225g/8oz 450g/1lb	Med.	5-5½ 6-7	Stir several times. Keep loosely covered.
Pork Chops	2 4	Med.	5 7½	Turn over halfway through. Cover loosely.
Lamb Chops	2 4	Med.	4-5 6-10	Turn over halfway through. Cover loosely.
Sliced beef, pork, veal	120g/4oz 225g/8oz	Med.	3-5 6-7½	Add gravy or sauce if possible. Cover loosely.
Sliced turkey, chicken, ham	120g/4oz 225g/8oz	Med.	2½-5 4-6	Add gravy or sauce if possible. Cover loosely.

	Quantity	Setting	Time from room temp. (minutes)	Special Instructions
Pasta	120g/4oz 225g/8oz	Med. or High	2-3 5-6	Stir once or twice. Add 5ml/ 1 tsp oil. Use shorter time for High setting.
Rice	120g/4oz 225g/8oz	Med. or High	2-3 4-5	Stir once or twice. Add 5ml/ 1 tsp oil or butter. Use shorter time for High setting.
Potatoes	120g/4oz 225g/8oz 450g/1lb	High	1-2 2-3 3-4	Use the shorter time for mashed potatoes. Do not reheat fried potatoes. Cover loosely.
Corn-on-the-Cob	2 ears 4 ears	High	2-3 4-6	Wrap in plastic wrap/cling film
Carrots	225g/8oz 450g/1lb	High	1-2 2-4	Cover loosely. Stir once.
Turnips	225g/8oz 450g/1lb	High	1-2 2-4	Cover loosely. Stir carefully.
Broccoli Asparagus	120g/4oz 225g/8oz	High	2 2	Cover loosely. Rearrange once.
Peas Beans Courgettes/ Zucchini	120g/4oz 225g/8oz	High	1-1½ 1½-2	Cover loosely. Stir occasionally.

To let air and heat circulate underneath breads, cakes and pastry shells, place them on a rack or inverted saucer. This allows the base to cook faster and more evenly. Once baked and cool, keep microwave-baked goods well covered. They seem to dry out faster than those conventionally baked.

Defrosting and Reheating

With the defrosting and reheating abilities of a microwave oven menu planning can become crisis-free. Most ovens incorporate an automatic defrosting control into their setting programs. If your oven does not have this facility, use the lowest temperature setting and employ an on/off technique. In other words, turn the oven on at 30 second-1 minute intervals and let the food stand for a minute or two before repeating the process. This procedure allows the food to defrost evenly without starting to cook at the edges. The times given in Charts No. 7 and 8 apply to ovens of 600-700 watts.

Always cover the food when defrosting or reheating. Plastic containers, plastic bags and freezer-to-table ware can be used to freeze and defrost food in. Meals can be placed on paper or plastic trays and frozen. Cover with cling film or greaseproof paper. Usually, foods are better defrosted first and cooked or reheated second. There are exceptions to this rule, so be sure to check instructions on pre-packaged foods before proceeding. Food frozen in blocks, such as spinach or casseroles, should be broken up as they defrost.

Breads, rolls and coffee cakes can be placed on paper plates or covered in paper towels to reheat or defrost. These materials will help protect the foods and absorb moisture which will come to the surface and could make these foods soggy. If you want a crisp crust on reheated bread, slip a sheet of foil under the paper towel and don't cover completely.

When reheating foods in a sauce, stir occasionally to distribute heat evenly. Spread food out in an even layer for uniform heating. Sauces and gravies can be poured over sliced meat and poultry to keep it moist while reheating. Vegetables, except for root vegetables and starchy ones like corn, lose texture when they are reheated. It is best to add them at the last

CHART 8 Defrosting

	Mins. on Low/ Defrost Setting per 450g/1lb	Mins. Stdg. Time	Instructions
Pork, Veal, Lamb, Beef for Roasting	8-10	30-40	Pierce covering. Turn frequently.
Ground/ Minced Beef or Lamb	7-8	5-6	Pierce wrapping. Break up as it defrosts.
Hamburgers	6-8	5	Use shorter time if individually wrapped. Pierce wrapper and separate when starting to defrost. Turn patties over once.
Bacon	6-8	5	Cover in paper towels. Separate as slices defrost.
Sausages	6-8	5	Cover in paper towels. Separate as defrosting.
Whole Chickens, Duck, Game Birds	5-7	30	Pierce wrapper. Remove giblets as soon as possible. Cover leg ends, wings, breast bone with foil part of the time. Turn several times.
Poultry Pieces	6-8	15-20	Pierce wrapper. Turn several times.
Casseroles, filled crêpes (for 4 people)	4-10	10	Defrost in dish, loosely covered. Stir casseroles if possible.

	Mins. on Low/ Defrost Setting per 450g/1lb	Mins. Stdg. Time	Instructions
Vegetables	1-8	3-5	Cover loosely. Break up or stir occasionally.
Fish Fillets and Steaks	6-10	5-10	Pierce wrapper. Separate during defrosting. Use greater time for steaks.
Whole Fish	6-8	10	Pierce wrapper. Turn over during defrosting. Cover tail with foil halfway through.
Shellfish	6-8	6	Pierce wrapper. Stir or break up pieces during defrosting.
Bread Loaf	2-4 (per average loaf)	5-10	Cover with paper towels. Turn over once.
1 Slice Bread	20 seconds	1	Cover in paper towels.
Rolls 6 12	1½-3 2-4	3 5	Cover in paper towels. Turn over once.
Cake	1½-2	2	Place on serving plate. Some icings not suitable.
Fruit Pie 23cm/9"	8-10	6	Use a glass dish. Place on inverted saucer or rack.

minute to other foods. To tell if reheating is completed, touch the bottom of the plate or container. If it feels hot, then the food is ready.

Foods can be arranged on plates in advance and reheated very successfully, an advantage when entertaining. With a microwave oven, you can spend more time with your guests than by yourself in the kitchen!

Recipe Conversion

Experiment with your favourite recipes and you will probably find that many of them can be converted for microwave cooking with only a few changes. Things that don't work are recipes which call for whipped egg whites, such as angel food cake and crisp meringue shells. Soft meringues for pies will work, and one of the most amazing recipe conversions is that for crisp meringues. These meringues triple in size as they cook and are made from a fondant-like mixture.

Batters for pancakes, waffles or Yorkshire pudding are impossible to cook successfully. Deep fat frying is understandably impossible. Yeast doughs and biscuit doughs must be specially formulated for microwave cooking. To convert your own recipes, the following rules will help:

* Look for similar microwave recipes with the same quantities of solid ingredients, dish size, techniques and times.

* Reduce liquid quantities by one quarter. More can always be added later in cooking.

* Cut down on fat and save calories as well as cooking time. Fat will attract microwave energy and slow down the cooking of the other ingredients in the recipe.

* Reduce the seasoning in your recipe; microwave cooking intensifies flavours.

* Microwave cooking takes approximately a quarter of the time of conventional cooking. Allow at least 5 minutes standing time before checking to see if the food is cooked. You can always add more time at this point if necessary.

Microwave
THE RECIPES

Microwave
THE RECIPES

Do meals for singles or couples have to be uninspiring? Do people on their own have to rely on pre-prepared food for speed and convenience? Not when there is a microwave around. Small portions cook beautifully in practically the time it takes to open the package and read the cooking instructions. With a microwave oven there is no need to sacrifice variety for convenience.

Small packages of fresh vegetables and meat are readily available in supermarkets and specialty food stores. Even turkey and duck are available in manageable sizes for the small household. Cooking a dinner party for one special guest can be cheaper than dinner out. It can also be an occasion for experimenting with more elaborate preparations than you might want to attempt for large numbers.

However, leftovers come in handy, so don't shy away from cooking a whole turkey or a large piece of meat. Leftovers can be frozen and used as a basis for completely different meals later on. Small portions, well covered, will defrost in 2-3 minutes on a LOW or DEFROST setting. Soups can be kept refrigerated for up to two days and reheated on MEDIUM in about 2-5 minutes. Vegetable and flour-thickened soups can also be frozen, and then defrosted and reheated in about 10 minutes on a LOW or DEFROST setting, with frequent stirring. Meat, poultry and game stews and braises can be reheated as well, usually on MEDIUM for about 4-6 minutes. If frozen, they can be defrosted and reheated in about 12-15 minutes on LOW or DEFROST. Individual portions should be frozen in bags or containers that are suitable for reheating in microwave ovens or in individual serving dishes of the freezer-to-table variety.

All the recipes in this book were tested in an oven with a maximum power of 700 watts. Certain recipes were cooked in a combination microwave-convection oven, which combines the speed of microwave cooking with browning ability. However, any dish that requires browning can be placed under a preheated broiler or grill for a minute or two before serving. Also, toppings such as breadcrumbs, crushed cereals or cheeses can give an eye-pleasing finish to your very own brand of 'convenience' food.

SOUPS AND APPETIZERS

Confetti Spread and Sesame Crackers

PREPARATION TIME: 15 minutes

MICROWAVE COOKING TIME:
10-12 minutes

SERVES: 2 people

SPREAD
225g/8oz/1 cup cream cheese
2 strips bacon, diced
15g/1 tbsp chopped chives
Red pepper flakes
4 chopped black olives
Crushed garlic
60g/2oz/¼ cup chopped green and red
  peppers, mixed
30g/1oz/2 tbsps frozen corn
Salt and pepper

CRACKERS/BISCUITS
60g/2oz/¼ cup all-purpose flour/plain
  flour
60g/2oz/¼ cup wholewheat flour/
  wholemeal flour
45g/1½ oz/1½ tbsps butter
10ml/2 tsps sesame seeds
15-30ml/1-2 tbsps cold water
1 egg, beaten with a pinch of salt
Salt and pepper

Put the flours, salt and pepper into the bowl of a food processor. Cut the butter into small pieces and add to the flour. Process until the mixture looks like fine breadcrumbs. Add 1 tbsp sesame seeds and add the water with the machine running until the mixture forms a dough. Roll out thinly on a floured board and brush with the egg. Sprinkle on the remaining sesame seeds and cut into 2.5cm (1") squares. Arrange into a circle on a large plate and cook on HIGH for 3-6 minutes until crisp.

Cool on a wire rack. Makes 12 crackers.
Heat a browning dish for 3 minutes and cook the diced bacon on HIGH for 1-2 minutes or until crisp. Drain on paper towels and allow to cool. Put the chopped peppers and corn into a small bowl and cover with water. Cover the bowl with pierced

This page: Confetti Spread with Sesame Crackers. Facing page: Oriental Kebabs.

plastic wrap and cook on HIGH for 2 minutes. Rinse with cold water and leave to drain dry. Put the cream cheese into a small bowl and heat for

30-40 seconds on MEDIUM to soften. Add the bacon, peppers and the remaining ingredients, and mix well. Serve with the sesame seed crackers. Unused peppers can be frozen.

Marinated Shrimp and Sour Cream Sauce

PREPARATION TIME: 15 minutes

MICROWAVE COOKING TIME:
5 minutes

SERVES: 2 people

225g/½ lb fresh large shrimp, shelled and cleaned

MARINADE
140ml/¼ pint/½ cup white wine
30ml/1oz/2 tbsps white wine vinegar
1 bay leaf
2 black peppercorns
1 whole allspice berry
2 whole cloves
2.5ml/½ tsp dill seeds
½ small onion, sliced
Salt

SAUCE
140ml/¼ pint/½ cup sour cream
30-45ml/2-3 tbsps strained reserved marinade
2.5ml/½ tsp chopped dill, fresh or dried
2.5ml/½ tsp grated horseradish
Salt and pepper

GARNISH
Lettuce leaves
Sprigs of fresh dill

Combine all the marinade ingredients in a 570ml/1 pint casserole and cover. Cook for 2-3 minutes on HIGH until boiling. Stir in the shrimp, cover, and cook on MEDIUM for 2 minutes. Allow to cool in the marinade. If using fresh dill, reserve 2 small sprigs for garnish and chop 2.5ml/½ tsp. Drain the marinade and mix with the sour cream, dill, horseradish, and salt and pepper. Arrange lettuce on serving plates, and place on the shrimp. Top with some of the sauce and the reserved dill. Serve remaining sauce separately.

Scallop Parcels with Curry Sauce

PREPARATION TIME: 15 minutes

MICROWAVE COOKING TIME:
3-4 minutes

SERVES: 2 people

6 large or 8 small scallops
1 small sweet red pepper
2 large mushrooms
30ml/1oz/2 tbsps white wine
5ml/1 tsp black pepper
1.5ml/¼ tsp salt
1.5ml/¼ tsp ground ginger
Garlic powder
15ml/1 tbsp oil
Whole fresh chives

SAUCE
15g/1 tbsp curry powder
140ml/¼ pint/½ cup plain yogurt
Juice of ½ a lime
2.5ml/½ tsp mango chutney
Salt and pepper

Mix the wine, salt, pepper, oil, ginger, and a pinch of garlic powder together well. Put in the scallops and turn them to coat evenly. Cut the pepper into pieces the size of the scallops. Cut the mushrooms into 5mm (¼") slices. Layer the pepper, mushrooms and scallops, and tie each parcel with 2 whole chives. Put the parcels on their sides onto a microwave roasting rack and cook on HIGH for 30 seconds. Turn every 30 seconds, ending with the parcels scallop-sides up. Cook for a total of 2-3 minutes, brushing frequently with the ginger basting liquid. Serve hot or cold, with the curry sauce.
Put the curry powder for the sauce onto a small plate and cook for 1 minute on HIGH. Allow to cool, and combine with the other ingredients. Serve with the scallops.

Oriental Kebabs

PREPARATION TIME: 20 minutes

MICROWAVE COOKING TIME:
5-6 minutes

SERVES: 2 people

90g/3oz ground/minced pork or beef
30g/1oz/2 tbsp breadcrumbs
5ml/1 tsp chopped onion
1 small can pineapple chunks
6 cherry tomatoes

BASTING MIXTURE
60ml/2oz/¼ cup honey
60ml/2oz/¼ cup soy sauce
60ml/2oz/¼ cup rice wine
15ml/1 tbsp sesame seed oil
5ml/1 tsp ground ginger
Pepper

SWEET AND SOUR SAUCE
Remaining basting mixture
15ml/1 tbsp ketchup
5ml/1 tsp cornstarch/cornflour
Reserved pineapple juice
15ml/1 tbsp cider vinegar
2.5ml/½ tsp garlic powder

Mix together the basting ingredients. Mix the meat, breadcrumbs, chopped onion and 1 tbsp of the basting mixture. Shape into 8 meatballs. Drain the can of pineapple and reserve the juice. Thread the meatballs onto wooden skewers, alternating with the pineapple chunks and tomatoes. Place the kebabs on a roasting rack and brush with the baste. Cook on HIGH for 3 minutes, turning and basting each minute. Combine the ingredients for the sauce, and cook on HIGH for 2-3 minutes until thickened. Stir every 30 seconds. Serve with the kebabs. For one person only, use half the amount of all the ingredients. Cook the kebabs for 2 minutes, and the sauce for 1-2 minutes.

Tomato and Basil Soup

PREPARATION TIME: 15 minutes

MICROWAVE COOKING TIME:
5 minutes

SERVES: 2 people

Facing page: Scallop Parcels with Curry Sauce (top) and Marinated Shrimp and Sour Cream Sauce (bottom).

700ml/1¼ pints/2 cups tomato sauce/
 tinned tomatoes, liquidized and sieved
280ml/½ pint/1 cup hot water
½ a beef bouillon stock cube, or 5ml/1 tsp
 instant beef bouillon granules
30ml/1oz/2 tbsps cream
30ml/1oz/2 tbsps red wine
1.25ml/¼ tsp cornstarch/cornflour
Pinch sugar
2 tbsps fresh basil leaves
2 tbsps parsley
½ clove garlic
30ml/1oz/2 tbsps olive oil
Salt and pepper

Mix the tomato sauce, water, beef
bouillon, sugar, and salt and pepper
together in a 1150ml/2 pint, 1 quart
casserole. Cover and cook for
2 minutes on HIGH. Mix the
cornstarch and wine together and stir
into the soup. Heat for 2 minutes on
HIGH, stirring every 30 seconds. Put
the basil leaves, parsley and garlic
into a blender and purée. Add the oil
in a thin, steady stream with the
machine running. Re-heat the soup
for 1 minute on HIGH, and stir in the
cream just before serving. Add the

basil mixture, and stir through the
soup.
To serve one person only, use half of
all the ingredients, and cook the soup
for a total of 2 minutes.

Consommé with Vegetable Noodles

PREPARATION TIME: 15 minutes

MICROWAVE COOKING TIME:
5 minutes

SERVES: 2 people

300g/10½ oz can condensed beef or
 chicken consommé
430ml/¾ pint/1½ cups water
1 bay leaf
15ml/½ oz/1 tbsp sherry
1 small zucchini/courgette
1 small carrot, peeled

Combine the consommé and the
water. Add the bay leaf and heat
through for 1 minute on HIGH. Cut
ends off the zucchini/courgette and
carrot, and using a swivel peeler, pare

the vegetables lengthwise into thin
strips. Add the carrot noodles to the
consommé, cover with pierced plastic
wrap, and cook on HIGH for
3 minutes. Add the zucchini/
courgette and cook for an additional
1 minute on HIGH. Stir in the sherry
before serving.

Cheesy Spinach Soup

PREPARATION TIME: 15 minutes

MICROWAVE COOKING TIME:
5 minutes

SERVES: 1 person

120g/4oz/½ cup frozen spinach
60g/2oz/½ cup shredded Red Leicester/
 Colby cheese
30ml/1oz/2 tbsps hot water
15g/½ oz/1 tbsp butter
15g/½ oz/1 tbsp flour/plain flour
½ a chicken bouillon/stock cube
15ml/1 tbsp chopped onion
280ml/½ pint/1 cup milk
Pinch of thyme
Pinch of nutmeg
Salt and pepper

Put the spinach, onion and water
into a small bowl and cover with
pierced plastic wrap. Cook for
1 minute on HIGH and set aside. Put
the butter into another bowl and
cook for 30 seconds on HIGH or
until melted. Add the flour, bouillon
cube, nutmeg, thyme, milk, and salt
and pepper. Cook on MEDIUM for
4 minutes or until thickened. Stir
frequently. Add the spinach and its
cooking liquid to the soup, and purée
in a food processor until smooth. Stir
in the cheese, reserving 1 tbsp.
Re-heat on MEDIUM for 1 minute.
Sprinkle the reserved cheese on top
to serve.
To serve 2 people, double the
ingredients and cook the soup for 5-6
minutes on MEDIUM.

**This page: Consommé with
Vegetable Noodles. Facing page:
Cheesy Spinach Soup (top) and
Tomato and Basil Soup (bottom).**

Microwave COOKING FOR 1 & 2

SNACKS

Italian Ham Sandwiches

PREPARATION TIME: 10 minutes

MICROWAVE COOKING TIME: 4 minutes

SERVES: 2 people

120g/¼ lb Parma, or other Italian ham
60g/2oz sliced Mozzarella cheese
4 mild Italian peppers
15g/½ oz/1 tbsp butter or margarine
Pinch garlic powder
Pinch of oregano
2 French rolls

Mix the butter, garlic and oregano. Split the rolls and spread the butter thinly on each of the cut sides. Layer the ham, peppers and cheese on the bottom half of the roll. Place the top on and press down. Place the sandwiches on a paper towel in the oven. Cook on MEDIUM for 4-5 minutes or until the cheese melts. Serve immediately.

Sloppy Joes

PREPARATION TIME: 15 minutes

MICROWAVE COOKING TIME: 14 minutes

SERVES: 2 people

225g/½ lb ground/minced beef or pork
1 small onion, finely chopped
60g/2oz/¼ cup chopped green pepper
280ml/½ pint/1 cup tomato sauce/
   canned tomatoes

This page: Italian Ham Sandwiches (top) and Cheese and Mushroom Croissants (bottom). Facing page: Sausage and Sauerkraut Sandwiches (top) and Sloppy Joes (bottom).

2 tsps Worcestershire sauce
½ tsp dry mustard
1½ tsps cider vinegar
1 tsp brown sugar
Salt and pepper
2 Kaiser rolls or hamburger buns

Mix the meat and onion in a casserole and cook, uncovered, for 7 minutes on HIGH. Mash the meat with a fork several times while cooking, to break it up into small pieces. Strain off any fat. Add the remaining ingredients and stir well. Cover and cook for a further 5 minutes on HIGH, stirring occasionally. Wrap the rolls in paper towels and heat for 1-2 minutes on MEDIUM. Split and fill with the Sloppy Joe filling. Mixture freezes well.

Tacos

PREPARATION TIME: 15 minutes

MICROWAVE COOKING TIME: 6 minutes

SERVES: 2 people

4 taco shells
120g/¼ lb ground/minced beef
60g/2oz/¼ cup chopped onion
15g/½ oz/1 tbsp raisins
15g/½ oz/1 tbsp pine nuts
15g/½ oz/1 tbsp corn/sweetcorn
5ml/1 tsp chili powder
60ml/2oz/¼ cup tomato sauce/canned
   tomatoes
Salt and pepper

TOPPINGS
60g/2oz/½ cup grated cheese
140ml/¼ pint/½ cup sour cream
120g/4oz/½ cup chopped tomatoes
60g/2oz/1 cup shredded lettuce
1 chopped avocado

Put the beef and onion into a 1150ml/2 pint/1 quart casserole. Break the meat up well with a fork. Cover and cook for 2 minutes on HIGH, stirring occasionally to break into small pieces. Drain any fat from the meat and add salt and pepper, chili powder, corn, nuts, raisins and tomato sauce. Cover and cook on MEDIUM for 4 minutes. Spoon into the taco shells and serve with the various toppings.

Sausage and Sauerkraut Sandwiches

PREPARATION TIME: 10 minutes

MICROWAVE COOKING TIME: 1½ minutes

SERVES: 2 people

4 slices rye bread, light or dark
120g/¼ lb smoked sausage (kielbasa or
   bratwurst), thinly sliced
4 slices Muenster or Tilsit cheese
90g/3oz/½ cup drained sauerkraut
30g/1oz/2 tbsps butter or margarine

DRESSING
15ml/1 tbsp spicy brown mustard
2 tbsps mayonnaise
7.5ml/1½ tsps chopped dill pickle

Melt the butter for 30 seconds on HIGH in a small bowl. Mix dressing and spread on both sides of the bread slices. Layer on the sauerkraut, sausage and cheese. Heat a browning dish for 5 minutes on HIGH. Brush 1 side of the bread with melted butter and place the sandwich in the dish. Cook for 15 seconds, or until golden brown. Turn over and brush the other side with butter and cook that side for 20-30 seconds or until the bread is browned and the cheese melted. Serve hot.

Cheese and Mushroom Croissants

PREPARATION TIME: 15 minutes

MICROWAVE COOKING TIME: 3 minutes

SERVES: 1 person

1 croissant or crescent roll
5ml/1 tsp butter
2.5ml/½ tsp flour/plain flour
2 mushrooms, sliced
60g/2oz/¼ cup Gruyère cheese
60ml/2oz/¼ cup milk
15ml/½ oz/1 tbsp white wine
2.5ml/½ tsp Dijon mustard
Nutmeg
Salt and pepper

Split the top of the croissant, taking care not to cut through to the bottom or the ends. Melt 2.5ml/½ tsp butter in a small bowl for 15 seconds on HIGH. Add the mushrooms and cook for 30 seconds on HIGH and set aside. Melt the remaining butter in a 570ml/1 pint measure. Stir in the flour and add the milk and wine gradually. Add a pinch of nutmeg, mustard and salt and pepper. Cook on HIGH for 1 minute or until thick. Stir in the cheese and spoon into the croissant. Top with the mushrooms and heat through for 1 minute on MEDIUM. Serve immediately.

Pizza Muffins

PREPARATION TIME: 10 minutes

MICROWAVE COOKING TIME: 2 minutes

SERVES: 1 person

1 English muffin, split
30ml/2 tbsps tomato paste
30ml/1oz/2 tbsps water
1 green/spring onion, sliced
1.25ml/¼ tsp oregano
Pinch garlic powder
60g/2oz/¼ cup pepperoni or Italian
   salami, chopped, or 4 anchovies
2-3 Italian olives, stoned and halved
5ml/1 tsp capers
45g/1½ oz/⅓ cup grated Mozzarella
   cheese
15g/½ oz/1 tbsp Parmesan cheese
Salt and pepper

Mix the tomato paste with the water, salt and pepper, onion, oregano and garlic powder, and spread on the muffin halves. Arrange the sausage or a cross of anchovies on top. Add the olives and capers and sprinkle on the Mozzarella cheese. Sprinkle on the Parmesan cheese last and put the pizzas on a paper towel, then cook for 1½-2 minutes on HIGH. Turn the pizzas once or twice during cooking. For 2 people, double the ingredients and cook for 4-4½ minutes on HIGH.

Facing page: Tacos.

Vegetable Pockets

| **PREPARATION TIME:** 10 minutes |
| **MICROWAVE COOKING TIME:** 4-5 minutes |
| **SERVES:** 2 people |

1 piece wholewheat pitta bread
15ml/½ oz/1 tbsp olive oil
5ml/1 tsp lemon juice
1 tomato, roughly chopped
1 red onion, thinly sliced or 2 green/spring
    onions, sliced
1 green pepper, thinly sliced
60g/2oz/1 cup fresh spinach leaves
2.5ml/½ tsp chives
15ml/1 tbsp fresh basil leaves, if available
1 small zucchini/courgette, thinly sliced
6 black olives, stoned
30g/1oz/¼ cup crumbled feta cheese
Salt and pepper

Cut the pitta bread in half and open
out the pockets. Mix the lemon juice
and oil together with the salt and
pepper. Toss the cheese, tomato,
vegetables, herbs and olives together
in the dressing. Fill the pockets with
the vegetables and heat for 4-5
minutes on MEDIUM. Serve
immediately.

Tuna Melt

| **PREPARATION TIME:** 10 minutes |
| **MICROWAVE COOKING TIME:** 2 minutes |
| **SERVES:** 1 person |

1 English muffin, split
1 small can white tuna
30ml/2 tbsps cottage cheese
30ml/2 tbsps mayonnaise
1 stick celery, chopped
5ml/1 tsp chopped parsley
10ml/2 tsps chopped chives
2.5ml/½ tsp lemon juice
Alfalfa sprouts
30g/1oz/¼ cup grated Colby/Red
    Leicester cheese
Salt and pepper

Mix together the tuna, cottage
cheese, mayonnaise, celery, parsley,
chives, and salt and pepper. Taste and
add lemon juice if desired. Put alfalfa
sprouts on the muffin halves and

spoon on the tuna mixture. Top with
the cheese and heat for 1 minute on
MEDIUM. Increase the heat to
HIGH and heat for 1 minute further,
turning once or twice during cooking.
Serve immediately.

Pocketful of Shrimp

| **PREPARATION TIME:** 10 minutes |
| **MICROWAVE COOKING TIME:** 2-4 minutes |
| **SERVES:** 2 people |

1 piece pitta bread, cut in half
60g/2oz/½ cup bean sprouts
120g/4oz/½ cup cooked shrimp, peeled
    and de-veined
15ml/1 tbsp chili sauce
30ml/1oz/2 tbsps mayonnaise
2.5ml/½ tsp horseradish

**This page: Pizza Muffins (top) and
Tuna Melt (bottom). Facing page:
Pocketful of Shrimp (top) and
Vegetable Pockets (bottom).**

1 stick celery, chopped
1 ripe avocado, peeled and thickly sliced
15ml/1 tbsp lemon juice
Salt and pepper

Cut the pitta bread in half and open
a pocket in each half. Toss the
avocado slices in lemon juice and
place them in the sides of the
pockets. Fill each pocket with bean
sprouts. Mix the shrimp, chili sauce,
mayonnaise, horseradish, salt, pepper
and chopped celery together. Put on
top of the bean sprouts and heat
through for 2-4 minutes on
MEDIUM. Serve immediately.

EGG AND CHEESE

Piperade

PREPARATION TIME: 10 minutes

MICROWAVE COOKING TIME:
6 minutes, plus 1 minute standing time

SERVES: 1 person

30ml/1 tbsp finely chopped onion
7.5gm/¼ oz/½ tbsp butter
½ cap pimento, finely chopped
1 tomato
Pinch garlic powder
2 eggs
Pinch oregano
Salt and pepper

Put 570ml/1 pint/2 cups water into a bowl and cover with pierced plastic wrap. Heat for 3 minutes on HIGH or until boiling. Put in the tomato and leave for 30 seconds. Peel and seed the tomato, and chop roughly. Put the butter into a medium-sized bowl with the garlic powder and onion. Cook on HIGH for 3 minutes. Add the pimento, tomato and oregano. Cook on HIGH for 1 minute. Beat the eggs, salt and pepper together, and add to the bowl. Cook on HIGH for about 2 minutes, stirring every 30 seconds, or until the eggs are softly scrambled. Leave to stand for 1 minute before serving. Serve on buttered toast or English muffins, or with French bread.

Sunrise Scramble

PREPARATION TIME: 15 minutes

MICROWAVE COOKING TIME:
5 minutes, plus 1 minute standing time

SERVES: 1 person

30g/1oz/2 tbsps ham, finely chopped
2 eggs
15g/½ oz/1 tbsp butter
15g/½ oz/1 tbsp grated cheese
30g/1oz/¼ cup mushrooms, sliced
1 tomato
15ml/1 tbsp chopped parsley
Salt and pepper

Put the butter into a small bowl, add the mushrooms, and cook for 2 minutes on HIGH or until soft. Drain away any excess liquid. Add the ham, and cook for 1 minute on HIGH. Cut the tomato in quarters, but leave attached at the base. Heat for 1 minute on HIGH, and keep warm. Beat the eggs and add the cheese, parsley, and salt and pepper. Add the eggs to the bowl with the ham and mushrooms, and cook for 2 minutes on HIGH, stirring every 30 seconds until softly scrambled. Leave to stand for 1 minute. Fill the tomato with the egg mixture and serve.

Spinach and Cheese Layered Quiche

PREPARATION TIME: 20 minutes

MICROWAVE COOKING TIME:
11-14 minutes, plus 6 minutes standing time

SERVES: 2 people

PASTRY
60g/2oz/⅓ cup all-purpose flour
60g/2oz/⅓ cup wholewheat/wholemeal flour
60g/2oz/¼ cup margarine
30g/1oz/2 tbsps shortening
60ml/2oz/¼ cup ice cold water
Pinch of salt

FILLING
60g/2oz/½ cup shredded Gruyère or Swiss cheese
3 eggs
60ml/2oz/¼ cup half and half/single cream
60g/2oz/¼ cup chopped frozen spinach, well drained
Nutmeg
Cayenne pepper or Tabasco
Salt and pepper

Put the flours, salt, margarine and shortening into the bowl of a food processor and work until the mixture resembles fine breadcrumbs. With the machine running, add the water gradually until the dough holds together. It may not be necessary to add all the water. Roll out the pastry on a floured board to 3mm (⅛") thick, and put into an 18cm (7") pie plate. Trim the edge and flute. Refrigerate for 10 minutes. Mix the eggs, cheese, half and half/cream and salt and pepper together well. Divide the mixture in half: add the spinach and pinch of nutmeg to one half, and a pinch of Cayenne pepper or a dash of Tabasco to the other. Prick the base of the pastry with a fork and cook on HIGH for 2-3 minutes or until it starts to crisp. Pour in the cheese mixture and cook for 4 minutes on MEDIUM, or until softly set. Leave to stand for 1 minute. Pour on the spinach mixture and cook for a further 7-10 minutes or until the center is softly set. Leave to stand for 6 minutes before serving.

Facing page: Sunrise Scramble (top) and Piperade (bottom).

Niçoise Eggs

PREPARATION TIME: 10 minutes

MICROWAVE COOKING TIME:
9 minutes

SERVES: 2 person

2 eggs
4 tomatoes, peeled, seeded and chopped
5ml/1 tsp butter
2 mushrooms, chopped
30ml/1oz/2 tbsps white wine
15ml/1 tbsp capers
4 black olives, stoned and sliced
2 anchovies, chopped
15ml/1 tbsp tarragon
Pinch of paprika
Salt and pepper
30g/1oz/¼ cup Gruyère or Swiss cheese,
   grated

**This page: Italian Fondue (left)
and Niçoise Eggs (right). Facing
page: Tuna and Tomato Quiche
(top) and Spinach and Cheese
Layered Quiche (bottom).**

Put the butter into a small casserole
and melt for 30 seconds on HIGH.
Add the chopped mushrooms,
tarragon and half the wine, and cook
for 2 minutes on HIGH. Add the
remaining ingredients except the
cheese, eggs and paprika, and cook
for 1-2 minutes on HIGH. Divide the
tomato mixture into 2 custard cups/
ramekin dishes and make a well in
the center. Put an egg into the center
of the mixture in each cup. Pierce the
yolk with a sharp knife. Pour over the
remaining wine. Cook for 3 minutes

on HIGH or until the white is set
and yolk is still soft. Sprinkle on the
cheese and paprika and cook for
1 minute on LOW to melt the
cheese.

Italian Fondue

PREPARATION TIME: 10 minutes

MICROWAVE COOKING TIME:
5 minutes

SERVES: 1 person

120g/4oz/1 cup shredded Mozzarella
   cheese
60g/2oz/½ cup shredded mild Cheddar
   cheese
5ml/1 tsp cornstarch/cornflour
90ml/3oz/⅓ cup red wine

15ml/1 tbsp tomato paste
5ml/1 tsp dry vermouth
½ clove garlic, crushed
2.5ml/½ tsp basil
2.5ml/½ tsp oregano
1 French roll, cut into cubes, or broccoli
    flowerets, carrot sticks and celery sticks

Toss the cheese and cornstarch to
mix. Put the wine into a deep bowl
and cook on MEDIUM for 1-2
minutes, or until it begins to bubble
– do not allow it to boil. Add the
remaining ingredients except the
bread (or vegetables), and stir well to
blend completely. Cook for a further
2-3 minutes on MEDIUM, or until
the cheese melts. Stir every few
seconds. If the mixture begins to boil,
reduce the setting to LOW. Serve
with the bread cubes or vegetables.
Re-heat on LOW if necessary. Serve
as an appetizer/starter or as an entrée
with a tossed salad.
To serve 2 people, double the
ingredients. Cook the wine for 2-3
minutes on MEDIUM, and the
cheese and other ingredients for 3-4
minutes on MEDIUM.

Tuna and Tomato Quiche

PREPARATION TIME: 20 minutes

MICROWAVE COOKING TIME:
18 minutes, plus 6 minutes standing
time

SERVES: 2 people

PASTRY
120g/4oz/⅔ cup all-purpose/plain flour
60g/2oz/¼ cup margarine
30g/1oz/2 tbsps shortening
30ml/1 tbsp paprika
Pinch of salt
60ml/2oz/¼ cup ice cold water

FILLING
1 can (about 180g/6oz) white tuna,
    drained and flaked
3 eggs
2 tomatoes, peeled
60g/2oz/½ cup shredded Cheddar
    cheese
60ml/2oz/¼ cup half and half/single
    cream
15ml/1 tbsp chopped green/spring onion
Salt and pepper

TOPPING
15ml/1 tbsp dry, seasoned breadcrumbs
30g/1oz/2 tbsps grated Parmesan cheese

Put the flour, salt, paprika, margarine
and shortening into the bowl of a
food processor and work until the
mixture resembles fine breadcrumbs.
With the machine running, add the
water gradually until the dough holds
together. It may not be necessary to
add all the water. Roll out the pastry
on a floured board to 3mm (⅛")
thick and put into an 18cm (7") pie
plate. Trim the edge and flute.
Refrigerate for 10 minutes. Beat the
eggs with the salt, pepper and half
and half/single cream. Add the
cheese, onion and tuna. Cut the
tomatoes into quarters and take out
the seeds. Prick the base of the pastry
and cook on HIGH for 2-3 minutes,
or until starting to crisp. Pour the
filling into the pastry shell and
decorate the top with the tomatoes.
Cook on MEDIUM for 10-15
minutes. Mix the topping ingredients
and sprinkle over the top of the
quiche 5 minutes before the end of
baking. Left-over quiche can be
refrigerated for up to 2 days. Eat cold
or re-heat on MEDIUM for
2 minutes.

Ham, Broccoli and Pineapple au Gratin

PREPARATION TIME: 15 minutes

MICROWAVE COOKING TIME:
10-12 minutes

SERVES: 2 people

4 slices cooked ham
8 broccoli spears
30g/1oz/¼ cup sliced mushrooms
15g/½ oz/1 tbsp butter
4 pineapple rings, drained
30ml/1oz/2 tbsps water
Pinch of salt
5ml/1 tsp dark brown sugar

SAUCE
15g/½ oz/1 tbsp flour/plain flour
15g/½ oz/1 tbsp butter
1.25ml/¼ tsp dry mustard
140ml/¼ pint/½ cup milk
30g/1oz/2 tbsps shredded Cheddar
   cheese
Salt and pepper

TOPPING
30g/1oz/¼ cup dry seasoned
   breadcrumbs

Put 15g/½ oz/1 tbsp butter in a small bowl and cook for 30 seconds on HIGH. Add the mushrooms and cook for 1 minute on HIGH and set aside. Put the broccoli spears into a casserole with the water and a pinch of salt. Cover and cook for 4 minutes on HIGH. Leave covered while preparing the sauce. In a 570ml/1 pint/ 2 cup measure, melt 15g/1oz/1 tbsp butter for 30 seconds on HIGH. Stir in the flour, mustard, salt and pepper. Add the milk gradually and cook on HIGH for 1-2 minutes, stirring frequently until thick. Stir in the cheese. Put 2 broccoli spears on each ham slice, stalks towards the middle, and top each with the mushrooms. Roll up and put seam-side down in a baking dish. Arrange pineapple rings on each side and sprinkle with the dark brown sugar. Coat the cheese sauce over the broccoli and ham rolls and top with the crumbs. Cook on MEDIUM for 3-4 minutes or until hot. Serve immediately.

To serve 1 person, make full quantity sauce and cut all other ingredients to half quantity. Cook the mushrooms for 30 seconds on HIGH and the broccoli for 3 minutes on HIGH. Once assembled, cook for 2-3 minutes on MEDIUM. Left-over cheese sauce can be frozen, or kept in the refrigerator for 2 days. Bring to room temperature, re-heat on MEDIUM for 1-2 minutes to serve the sauce.

Asparagus and Tomato Omelette

PREPARATION TIME: 15 minutes

MICROWAVE COOKING TIME: 15 minutes

SERVES: 2 people

4 eggs, separated
120g/4oz/½ cup chopped asparagus,
   fresh or frozen
30ml/1oz/2 tbsps water
2 tomatoes, peeled, seeded and chopped
45g/1½ oz/⅓ cup Gruyère cheese, grated
90ml/3oz/⅓ cup milk
15g/½ oz/1 tbsp butter or margarine
5ml/1 tsp flour/plain flour
Salt and pepper

Put the asparagus and water into a 570ml/1 pint casserole. Cover and cook for 5-6 minutes on HIGH. Beat the egg yolks, milk, flour, and salt and pepper together. Beat the egg whites until stiff but not dry and fold into the yolks. Melt the butter in a 23cm (9") pie plate for 30 seconds on HIGH. Pour the omelette mixture onto the plate and cook on MEDIUM for 7 minutes or until set. Lift the edges of the omelette to allow the uncooked mixture to spread evenly. Sprinkle with the cheese, and spread on the asparagus and chopped tomato. Fold over and cook for 1 minute on LOW to melt the cheese. Serve immediately.

This page: Ham, Broccoli, and Pineapple au Gratin. Facing page: Asparagus and Tomato Omelette.

Egg Foo Yung

PREPARATION TIME: 15 minutes

MICROWAVE COOKING TIME:
10 minutes

SERVES: 2 people

CRAB PATTIES
*120g/4oz/½ cup frozen crabmeat,
   defrosted*
15ml/1 tbsp chopped green pepper
*15ml/1 tbsp chopped green onion/spring
   onion*

30g/1oz/¼ cup chopped mushrooms
1 small clove garlic, crushed
60g/2oz/½ cup beansprouts
2 eggs, beaten
1.25ml/¼ tsp ground ginger
Salt and pepper

SAUCE
140ml/¼ pint/½ cup chicken bouillon
5ml/1 tsp sherry
15ml/1 tbsp soy sauce
5ml/1 tsp oyster sauce (optional)
2.5ml/½ tsp brown sugar
10ml/2 tsps cornstarch/cornflour

Beat the eggs in a medium-sized bowl
and stir in the remaining ingredients
for the patties. Cook on HIGH for
2 minutes, stirring frequently, until
softly set. Heat a browning dish on
HIGH for 5 minutes. Pour the
mixture into the hot dish in 140ml/
¼ pint/½ cup amounts, and cook for
about 30 seconds per side on HIGH.
Cover and keep warm. Combine the
sauce ingredients in a 570ml/1 pint/
2 cup measure and cook for 1-2
minutes, stirring frequently until
clear and thickened. Pour over the
patties and serve immediately.

RICE, PASTA AND GRAINS

Bulgur and Spicy Lamb

PREPARATION TIME: 20 minutes

MICROWAVE COOKING TIME:
26 minutes

SERVES: 2 people

120g/4oz/1 cup bulgur wheat
280ml/½ pint/1 cup water
1 small onion, finely chopped
120g/4oz/¼ lb ground/minced lamb
2.5ml/¼ tsp oil
225g/8oz/1 cup canned plum tomatoes
5ml/1 tsp cumin
1.25ml/¼ tsp cinnamon
5ml/1 tsp chopped mint
30g/1oz/2 tbsps raisins
30g/1oz/2 tbsps almonds, chopped
60ml/2oz/¼ cup yogurt
1 egg
Salt and pepper
1 bay leaf

Put the bulgur and water into a
2 quart casserole with a pinch of salt.
Cover and cook on HIGH for
5 minutes, and leave covered while
preparing the rest of the ingredients.
Heat a browning dish for 5 minutes
on HIGH. Put in the oil, add the
onion and lamb, breaking the latter
up into small pieces with a fork. Add
the cumin, cinnamon, and salt and
pepper. Return the dish to the oven
and cook for 5 minutes on HIGH,
stirring frequently. Add the tomatoes,
mint, bay leaf, and salt and pepper.
Cover and cook for 5 minutes on
HIGH. Add the raisins and almonds,
and leave to stand. Drain the bulgur
wheat well, pressing to remove excess
moisture. Mix with the egg and
yogurt. Add salt and pepper and put
half the bulgur in the bottom of a
baking dish. Spread with the lamb
filling and cover with another layer of
bulgur. Cook uncovered for 5-6
minutes on MEDIUM. Leave to
stand, to firm up, for 5 minutes
before serving. Serve with a
cucumber and yogurt salad.

**Facing page: Egg Foo Yung. This
page: Polenta with Pepper and
Leek Salad (top) and Bulgur and
Spicy Lamb (bottom).**

To serve 1 person, prepare the full quantity casserole and divide into two. One of the casseroles may be frozen.

Sausage Risotto

PREPARATION TIME: 15 minutes

MICROWAVE COOKING TIME: 29 minutes

SERVES: 2 people

60g/2oz/½ cup Italian rice, uncooked
30g/1oz/¼ cup broken, uncooked spaghetti
1 Italian sausage, mild or hot
15ml/1 tbsp oil
1 small onion, finely sliced
½ clove garlic, crushed
60g/2oz/½ cup quartered mushrooms
2 tomatoes, peeled and seeded
7.5ml/1½ tsps chopped parsley
2.5ml/½ tsp basil
280ml/½ pint/1 cup beef bouillon
60g/2oz/¼ cup Parmesan cheese
Salt and pepper

Remove sausage meat from casing. Heat a browning dish for 5 minutes on HIGH. Add the oil and sausage. Cook for 4 minutes on HIGH, breaking up the sausage meat with the fork. Add the onion, garlic and mushrooms, and cook for 2 minutes more on HIGH, stirring frequently. Put the contents of the browning dish into a 1150ml/2 pint/1 quart casserole and add the rice, spaghetti, basil, salt and pepper, and beef bouillon. Cover and cook for 15 minutes on HIGH. Stir in the parsley and chopped tomatoes, and leave to stand 3 minutes before serving. Sprinkle with Parmesan cheese.

Tri-colored Tagliatelle and Vegetables

PREPARATION TIME: 10 minutes

MICROWAVE COOKING TIME: 12 minutes, plus 2 minutes standing time

SERVES: 1 person

60g/2oz tagliatelle or fettucini (mixture of red, green and plain)
½ a small sweet red pepper, cut into 5mm (¼") strips
½ a small onion, thinly sliced
60g/2oz/½ cup broccoli flowerets
30g/1oz/2 tbsps butter
1 small clove garlic, crushed
7.5ml/1½ tsps dried rosemary (or 1 sprig fresh)
Grated Parmesan cheese
Salt and pepper

Put the pasta into a large bowl and cover with water. Cook for 6 minutes on HIGH. Leave to stand for 2 minutes. Rinse in hot water and leave to drain. If using fresh pasta, cut the cooking time in half. Put 15g/½ oz/ 1 tbsp butter into a medium-sized

This page: Sausage Risotto. Facing page: Tri-colored Tagliatelle and Vegetables.

bowl and add the broccoli, onion and red pepper strips. Cover with pierced plastic wrap and cook for 1-2 minutes on HIGH. Toss with the pasta and keep warm. Melt the remaining butter with the crushed garlic and rosemary for 30 seconds on HIGH in a small bowl or custard cup/ramekin dish. Strain the butter onto the pasta and vegetables and discard the rosemary and garlic. Season with salt and pepper. Heat the pasta through on MEDIUM for 2 minutes. Toss with

Parmesan cheese and serve. For 2 people, double all the ingredients. Cook the pasta for 10 minutes on HIGH if using dried, and 5 minutes on HIGH if using fresh. Cook the broccoli, onion and red pepper for 2-3 minutes on HIGH.

Polenta with Pepper and Leek Salad

PREPARATION TIME: 15 minutes

MICROWAVE COOKING TIME: 12 minutes, plus 5 minutes standing time

SERVES: 2 people

120g/4oz/½ cup yellow cornmeal
420ml/¾ pint/1½ cups water
15ml/1 tbsp finely chopped onion
30g/1oz/¼ cup shredded Mozzarella cheese
60g/2oz/¼ cup Parmesan cheese
Salt and pepper

SALAD
1 red pepper
1 large or 2 small leeks

DRESSING
15ml/1 tbsp vinegar
30ml/2 tbsps oil
2.5ml/½ tsp dry mustard
1.25ml/¼ tsp sugar
1.25ml/¼ tsp fennel seeds, crushed
1.25ml/¼ tsp marjoram

Mix the cornmeal, salt and pepper, onion and water in a large bowl. Cook for 6 minutes on HIGH. Add the Mozzarella, cover and leave to stand for 5 minutes. Spread into a square pan and sprinkle the top with the Parmesan cheese. Refrigerate, and when ready to use, cut into squares and heat for 1 minute on HIGH before serving. Slice the pepper into 5mm (¼″) strips. Trim off the dark green tops of the leeks and slice the white part into quarters. Mix the dressing ingredients together and put the vegetables into a 1 pint casserole. Pour over the dressing and mix together well. Cover and cook for 5 minutes on MEDIUM. Serve warm with the polenta.

Barley Ring with Turkey Filling

PREPARATION TIME: 20 minutes

MICROWAVE COOKING TIME: 31 minutes, plus 5 minutes standing time

SERVES: 2 people

120g/4oz/1 cup pearl barley
850ml/1½ pints/3 cups water
1 egg, beaten
60g/2oz/½ cup whole cranberries
2.5ml/½ tsp sugar
Grated rind and juice of half an orange
60g/2oz/½ cup chopped walnuts
30g/1oz/2 tbsps butter or margarine
1 shallot
90g/3oz/¾ cup mushrooms, sliced
225g/8oz/½ lb uncooked boned turkey, cut into 2.5cm (1″) pieces
15g/½ oz/1 tbsp flour/plain flour
140ml/¼ pint/½ cup chicken bouillon/ stock
30ml/2 tbsps parsley
140ml/¼ pint/½ cup cream
Salt and pepper

Put the barley into a large bowl with the water and a pinch of salt. Cover with pierced plastic wrap and cook for 20 minutes on HIGH, stirring once. Leave to stand, covered, for at least 5 minutes. Combine the cranberries, sugar and orange juice in a small bowl. Cook uncovered for 1-2 minutes on HIGH. Drain the barley well, and fold in the parsley, cranberries, walnuts, orange rind and beaten egg. Press into a 570ml/ 1 pint/2 cup microwave ring-mold. Put the butter into a 570ml/1 pint/ 2 cup casserole and cook for 30 seconds on HIGH to melt. Add the turkey, shallot and mushrooms. Cover and cook for 2 minutes on HIGH, stirring every 30 seconds. Sprinkle on the flour and stir in well. Add the stock and cream and blend well. Season, cover and cook for an additional 3 minutes on HIGH, stirring every 30 seconds until thickened. Keep warm. Re-heat the barley ring covered with pierced plastic wrap for 3 minutes on HIGH. Turn it out and fill the center with the turkey.
To serve one person, cut all the

ingredients to half quantity, and omit the egg. Serve the barley as a pilaff topped with the turkey filling.

Indian Pilaff

PREPARATION TIME: 15 minutes

MICROWAVE COOKING TIME: 30 minutes

SERVES: 2 people

60g/2oz/½ cup long-grain rice (basmati, if available)
30g/1oz/¼ cup almonds, toasted
1 small onion, sliced
15ml/1 tbsp oil
30g/1oz/2 tbsps peas
2 okra, sliced
30g/1oz/2 tbsps coconut
30g/1oz/2 tbsps golden raisins
280ml/½ pint/1 cup chicken bouillon
15ml/1 tbsp lemon juice
15ml/1 tbsp curry powder
15ml/1 tbsp chopped parsley
2.5ml/½ tsp dried red pepper flakes
Salt and pepper

Heat a browning dish for 5 minutes on HIGH. Sprinkle on the almonds and return the dish to the oven. Cook on HIGH for 3 minutes, stirring the almonds every 30 seconds until golden brown. Remove the almonds from the dish and allow to cool. Add the oil to the browning dish and stir in the sliced onion. Return to the oven and cook for 2 minutes on HIGH or until golden brown. Add the curry powder and cook for 1 minute on HIGH. Put the onion into a casserole and add the rice, pepper flakes, coconut, chicken bouillon and lemon juice. Cover and cook on HIGH for 3 minutes until boiling. Reduce the setting to MEDIUM, add the raisins and cook for 12 minutes. Add the peas, okra and parsley 2 minutes before the end of the cooking time. Sprinkle with toasted almonds before serving. (One serving may be kept in the refrigerator for 2 days. Re-heat for 2-3 minutes on MEDIUM.)

Facing page: Barley Ring with Turkey Filling.

Fried Rice

PREPARATION TIME: 15 minutes

MICROWAVE COOKING TIME: 12 minutes

SERVES: 2 people

60g/2oz/½ cup quick-cooking rice
200ml/6oz/¾ cup water
3 dried Chinese mushrooms
2 green/spring onions, sliced
60g/2oz/¼ cup shrimp, peeled and de-
 veined
Small piece ginger root
Small can sliced bamboo shoots or lotus
 root
1 egg
7.5ml/1½ tsps soy sauce
2.5ml/½ tsp sesame oil
1 tbsp vegetable oil
Salt and pepper

Put the mushrooms into a bowl with enough water to cover. Cover with pierced plastic wrap and cook for 3 minutes on HIGH. Leave to stand until softened. Put the rice, water and a pinch of salt in a 150ml/2 pint/ 1 quart casserole. Cover and cook on HIGH for 2½ minutes. Leave to stand while preparing the other ingredients. Drain and slice the mushrooms. Slice the ginger into thin slivers. Beat the egg with the soy sauce. Heat a browning dish for 5 minutes on HIGH, pour in the vegetable oil and quickly add the mushrooms, bamboo shoots, ginger, and half the onion. Stir and return to the oven, and cook for 1 minute on HIGH. Mix the rice with the egg, soy sauce and sesame oil, and stir into the mixture in the browning dish. Cook, uncovered, for 3 minutes on HIGH, stirring every 30 seconds until the egg sets. Add the shrimp after 2 minutes. Serve garnished with the remaining green onion.

Clam Shells in Saffron Sauce

PREPARATION TIME: 15 minutes

MICROWAVE COOKING TIME: 16 minutes, plus 5 minutes standing time

SERVES: 2 people

120g/4oz/1½ cups wholewheat
225g/8oz/1 cup canned whole clams,
 liquid reserved
30ml/2 tbsps chopped parsley
1-2 tomatoes, peeled, seeded and cut into
 5mm (¼") strips
1 shallot, finely chopped
15ml/1 tbsp saffron
15g/½ oz/1 tbsp butter
7ml/½ tbsp flour/plain flour
140ml/¼ pint/½ cup heavy/double
 cream
Reserved clam juice, made up to 140ml/

¼ pint/½ cup with water if necessary
30ml/1oz/2 tbsps white wine
Salt and pepper

Put the pasta shells into a large bowl with enough hot water to cover. Cook for 8 minutes on HIGH and leave to stand for 5 minutes. Rinse under hot water and leave in cold water. Melt the butter in a small bowl on HIGH for 30 seconds. Stir in the flour and add the clam juice gradually. Add the wine, shallot and saffron and cook, covered with

SAUCE
345g/12oz/1½ cups canned plum
    tomatoes
15ml/1 tbsp oil
60g/12oz/½ cup sliced mushrooms
½ clove garlic, crushed
1.25ml/¼ tsp basil
Pinch ground allspice
5ml/1 tsp tomato paste
1 bay leaf
Salt and pepper

FILLING
120g/4oz/½ cup frozen chopped spinach,
    defrosted
60g/2oz/¼ cup pepperoni sausage,
    skinned and chopped
120g/4oz/1 cup ricotta cheese
60g/2oz/¼ cup grated Parmesan cheese
    (plus extra for serving if desired)
Nutmeg
Salt and pepper

Put the cannelloni or large shell pasta
into a large, shallow casserole, and
pour over enough hot water to cover.
Cook for 8 minutes on HIGH. Leave
to stand for 5 minutes. Rinse in hot
water and leave standing in cold
water. Put the oil into a 1 quart
casserole and heat for 30 seconds on
HIGH. Add the mushrooms and
garlic and cook for 1 minute on
HIGH. Add the remaining sauce
ingredients, cover, and cook for
5 minutes on HIGH. Stir well and
mash the tomatoes to break them up.
Meanwhile drain the pasta well. Mix
the filling ingredients together and fill
the pasta. Put the pasta into a small
casserole dish and pour over the
tomato sauce. Cook on HIGH for
5 minutes to heat through. Serve
with additional Parmesan cheese.
To serve one person, halve the
quantity of each ingredient. Cook the
sauce for 3 minutes total in a smaller
casserole or bowl. Alternatively,
prepare this recipe in full and freeze
one half for later use.

**Facing page: Indian Pilaff (top)
and Fried Rice (bottom). This
page: Clam Shells in Saffron
Sauce (top) and Cannelloni Stuffed
with Spinach, Cheese and
Pepperoni (bottom).**

pierced plastic wrap, for 3 minutes
on HIGH until thickened. Stir every
30 seconds. Stir in the cream and
cook for 1 minute on HIGH. Mix in
the clams, parsley, and salt and
pepper. Cover and cook for 2
minutes on HIGH to heat through.
Add the tomato strips and cook for
1 minute on MEDIUM. Pour over
the pasta and serve immediately.
To serve 1 person, cut the quantity of
all the ingredients by half. Cook the
sauce for half of the recommended
time.

Cannelloni Stuffed with Spinach, Cheese and Pepperoni

PREPARATION TIME: 15 minutes

MICROWAVE COOKING TIME:
19 minutes, plus 5 minutes
standing time

SERVES: 2 people

6-8 (depending on size) cannelloni or
    large shell pasta

FISH AND SEAFOOD

Stuffed Trout

PREPARATION TIME: 15 minutes

MICROWAVE COOKING TIME: 5 minutes

SERVES: 1 person

1 whole rainbow trout, cleaned
1 shallot, finely chopped
120g/4oz/½ cup frozen chopped spinach, thawed
Pinch of nutmeg
90g/3oz/¼ cup flaked crabmeat
15g/½ oz/1 tbsp chopped hazelnuts
1 cap pimento, chopped
30ml/1oz/2 tbsps heavy/double cream
15ml/½ oz/1 tbsp lemon juice
Paprika
Salt and pepper

Put the spinach, nutmeg and shallot into a small bowl. Cover with pierced plastic wrap and cook for 1 minute on HIGH to soften the shallot. Stir in the crab, nuts, paprika, salt, pepper, pimento and cream. Trim the tail and fins of the trout, and spoon the stuffing into the cavity. Sprinkle with lemon juice and cook in a shallow baking dish covered with pierced plastic wrap for 4 minutes on HIGH. Peel the skin off the body of the trout, but leave on the head and tail. Garnish with lemon if desired.

Salmon Steaks Bernaise

PREPARATION TIME: 10 minutes

MICROWAVE COOKING TIME: 4-5 minutes

SERVES: 1 person

1 salmon steak
15ml/½ oz/1 tbsp lemon juice
Salt and pepper
SAUCE
2 egg yolks
5ml/1 tsp tarragon or white wine vinegar
5ml/1 tsp lemon juice
5ml/1 tsp chopped tarragon
5ml/1 tsp chopped parsley
Cayenne pepper
60g/2oz/¼ cup butter, melted

This page: Portuguese Seafood Stew. Facing page: Salmon Steaks Bernaise (top) and Stuffed Trout (bottom).

Have a bowl of ice water ready. Combine the egg yolks, vinegar, lemon juice and herbs in a 570ml/ 1 pint glass measure. In a small bowl, melt the butter for 1 minute on HIGH until very hot. Whisk it into the egg yolks. Cook on HIGH for 15

seconds and whisk again. Repeat the process until the sauce is thick: this usually takes about 2 minutes. Put immediately into the bowl of ice water to stop the cooking. Add the Cayenne pepper, and salt if necessary. If the sauce begins to curdle, put the measure immediately into ice water and beat vigorously. Put the fish into a small baking dish with salt and pepper and lemon juice. Cover with pierced plastic wrap and cook on MEDIUM for 2-3 minutes. Leave to stand, covered, while making the sauce.

Flounder with Avocado

PREPARATION TIME: 15 minutes

MICROWAVE COOKING TIME:
8 minutes

SERVES: 2 people

225g/½ lb flounder fillets, skinned
1 small ripe avocado
30ml/1oz/2 tbsps cream cheese
5ml/1 tsp chives
Juice of 1 lime (or of half a lemon)
15ml/½ oz/1 tbsp white wine
5ml/1 tsp butter
2.5ml/½ tsp flour/plain flour
140ml/¼ pint/½ cup heavy/double cream
Salt and pepper

GARNISH
Reserved chives
Reserved avocado slices

Reserve 2-4 thin slices of avocado and brush with the lemon or lime juice. Mash the rest of the avocado with the cream cheese, chives, salt and pepper, and 5ml/1 tsp lime or lemon juice. Spread the filling over the fish and fold each fillet in half. Put the fillets in a shallow casserole and pour over the wine and remaining juice. Cover with pierced plastic wrap and cook for 6 minutes on MEDIUM. Keep warm. In a small bowl, melt the butter for 30 seconds on HIGH and stir in the flour. Strain on the cooking liquid from the fish and add the cream. Cook, uncovered, for 2 minutes on HIGH until thickened. Remove the fish to

serve on plates and pour some of the sauce over each fillet. Garnish with the reserved avocado slices and chives.

Lemon and Almond Sole

PREPARATION TIME: 10 minutes

MICROWAVE COOKING TIME:
11 minutes

SERVES: 2 people

2 whole sole fillets
1 lemon
30g/1oz/2 tbsps butter
60g/2oz/½ cup almonds
30g/1oz/¼ cup cornflake crumbs
2-4 parsley sprigs
Salt and pepper

Cut 4 thin slices from the lemon and squeeze the rest for juice. Cut 2 circles of baking parchment/unwaxed paper and grease with 15g/½ oz/ 1 tbsp butter. Lay on the fillets of fish and sprinkle over the lemon juice, salt and pepper. Seal up the parcels by twisting the open edges of the paper together. Cook for 5 minutes on MEDIUM. Heat a browning dish on HIGH for 4 minutes and add the remaining butter. Stir in the almonds and cook for 2 minutes, stirring frequently until brown. Stir in the cornflake crumbs. Open the parcels to serve and spoon on the almond topping. Garnish with reserved lemon slices and parsley.

Portuguese Seafood Stew

PREPARATION TIME: 15 minutes

MICROWAVE COOKING TIME:
11 minutes

SERVES: 2 people

3 tomatoes, chopped
½ a green pepper, chopped
½ cup canned clams, in shells if possible, and liquid
1 cod fillet (about 120g/¼ lb), cut into 5cm (2") pieces
1 red snapper fillet (about 120g/¼ lb), cut into 5cm (2") pieces

4 large raw shrimp/prawns, peeled and de-veined, or 60g/2oz/½ cup small shrimp/prawns
½ a clove garlic, chopped
60g/2oz/¼ cup chopped onion
2 tbsps olive oil
5ml/1 tsp tomato paste
30ml/1 tbsp chopped parsley
6 chopped black olives
140ml/¼ pint/½ cup white wine
1 potato, cut into 2.5cm (1") pieces
Salt and pepper

Put the cod and snapper into a casserole. Put the olive oil into another casserole with the onion and garlic and heat for 1 minute on HIGH. Add the potatoes, liquid from the clams, and the wine. Cover and cook for 6 minutes on HIGH. Stir in the tomato paste, add the fish and peppers, and cook for 2 minutes on HIGH. Add the shrimp and cook a further minute on HIGH. Add the tomatoes, clams and olives and cook for another minute on HIGH. Season, and garnish with chopped parsley.

Macadamia Fillets

PREPARATION TIME: 10 minutes

MICROWAVE COOKING TIME:
5 minutes

SERVES: 2 people

2 sole or flounder fillets
1 small can pineapple chunks
¼ of a green pepper, cut into 5mm (¼") strips
1 green/spring onion, shredded
30g/1oz/⅓ cup Macadamia nuts, roughly chopped

SAUCE
Reserved pineapple juice
15ml/½ oz/1 tbsp honey
10ml/2 tsps soy sauce
15ml/½ oz/1 tbsp vinegar
1.25ml/¼ tsp dry mustard
1 tsp cornstarch/cornflour

Facing page: Flounder with Avocado (top) and Lemon and Almond Sole (bottom).

Drain the pineapple and set aside the chunks. Mix the juice and the other sauce ingredients together in a bowl. Add the green pepper and cook uncovered for 1-2 minutes on HIGH or until thickened, stirring every 30 seconds. Add the pineapple chunks, nuts and onions, and set aside. Put the fish into a shallow casserole, thinner portion towards the center of the dish. Cover with pierced plastic wrap, and cook for 2 minutes on HIGH. Allow to stand for 30 seconds. Remove carefully to serving dishes. Coat with the Macadamia sauce. Serve with fried rice or stir-fried vegetables.

This page: Shrimp and Broccoli au Gratin. Facing page: Macadamia Fillets.

Shrimp and Broccoli au Gratin

PREPARATION TIME: 10 minutes
MICROWAVE COOKING TIME: 6 minutes
SERVES: 2 people

120g/4oz/1 cup broccoli flowerets
225g/½ lb large cooked shrimp, peeled and de-veined
30g/1oz/2 tbsps Parmesan cheese
15g/½ oz/1 tbsp dry breadcrumbs
5ml/1 tsp paprika

SAUCE
30g/1oz/2 tbsps Cheddar cheese
15g/½ oz/1 tbsp butter
15g/½ oz/1 tbsp flour/plain flour
140ml/¼ pint/½ cup milk
Pinch of dry mustard
Pinch of Cayenne pepper
Salt and pepper

Melt 15g/1 tbsp butter in a small

140ml/¼ pint/½ cup heavy/double cream

Melt the butter in a 570ml/1 pint casserole for 30 seconds on HIGH and add the shallot. Cook for 1 minute on HIGH, add the flour, white wine and saffron, and stir well to mix. Add the scallops (cut in half if large) and cook for 1-2 minutes on HIGH. Stir in the cream, parsley and pepper, and cook for a further 2 minutes on HIGH. Serve on parsley rice.

Lobster in Sherry Cream

PREPARATION TIME: 20 minutes

MICROWAVE COOKING TIME: 4 minutes

SERVES: 2 people

1 whole large lobster, boiled; or 1 large lobster tail
60g/2oz/½ cup sliced mushrooms
2.5ml/½ tsp celery salt
140ml/¼ pint/½ cup heavy/double cream
30ml/1oz/2 tbsps sherry
2.5ml/½ tsp butter
2.5ml/½ tsp flour/plain flour
60g/2oz/½ cup Gruyère cheese
Paprika
Pepper

Crack the lobster claws and remove the meat. Remove the meat from the tail, and combine. Reserve the empty tail shell to cook in if desired. Melt the butter for 15 seconds on HIGH, and add the mushrooms. Cook for 1 minute on HIGH and add the flour, sherry, cream, celery salt, and pepper. Cook for 2 more minutes on HIGH until thick, stirring frequently. Add the lobster and spoon into the shell, or a baking dish. Sprinkle on the cheese and plenty of paprika. Cook for 2 minutes on HIGH. Serve immediately.

This page: Scallops in Saffron Cream (top) and Lobster in Sherry Cream (bottom). Facing page: Orange Glazed Lamb Chops with Glazed Vegetables.

bowl for 30 seconds on HIGH. Stir in the flour, mustard and Cayenne pepper. Add the milk gradually until smooth. Cook for 1-2 minutes on HIGH, stirring every 30 seconds. Add salt and pepper and stir in the Cheddar cheese. Cover and set aside. Put the broccoli in a small bowl with 30ml/1oz/2 tbsps water. Cover with pierced plastic wrap and cook for 3 minutes on HIGH until almost tender. In individual dishes or 1 large baking dish, scatter over the broccoli and shrimp. Coat over the sauce, and sprinkle on the Parmesan cheese, crumbs and paprika. Heat through for 1-2 minutes on HIGH before serving.

Scallops in Saffron Cream

PREPARATION TIME: 10 minutes

MICROWAVE COOKING TIME: 8 minutes

SERVES: 2 people

340g/12oz/2 cups uncooked scallops (or 180g/6oz/1 cup, if very large)
1 shallot, finely chopped
1 small red pepper cut into 5mm (¼") strips
5ml/1 tsp parsley
5ml/1 tsp saffron
140ml/¼ pint/½ cup white wine
25g/¾ oz/1½ tbsps butter
25g/¾ oz/1½ tbsps flour/plain flour

MEAT, POULTRY AND GAME

Orange Glazed Lamb Chops with Glazed Vegetables

PREPARATION TIME: 20 minutes

MICROWAVE COOKING TIME: 14 minutes

SERVES: 2 people

2 lamb shoulder chops
140ml/¼ pint/½ cup orange juice
10ml/2 tsps dark corn syrup
2.5ml/½ tsp red wine vinegar or cider vinegar
2.5ml/½ tsp cornstarch/cornflour
15ml/½ oz/1 tbsp water
15ml/½ oz/1 tbsp oil
1 carrot, cut into thick barrel shapes
1 turnip, quartered
60g/2oz/½ cup small onions
1 small potato, quartered
15g/½ oz/1 tbsp butter
Salt and pepper

GARNISH
Orange slices

Heat a browning dish for 5 minutes on HIGH. Put in the oil and chops and cook for 2 minutes on HIGH, turning once, until lightly browned on both sides. Transfer the chops to a casserole dish. Melt the butter and add the vegetables. Cook for 5 minutes on HIGH, stirring frequently to brown evenly. Add to the casserole dish with the chops. De-glaze the browning dish with the orange juice and vinegar, scraping any sediment off the base of the dish. Stir in the corn syrup, salt and pepper, and pour over the chops and vegetables. Cover with pierced plastic wrap and cook on MEDIUM for 6 minutes, or until chops are cooked as much as desired. The chops may be served slightly pink. Remove the chops and vegetables from the casserole and dissolve the cornstarch/cornflour in the water. Stir into the liquid in the casserole and cook, uncovered, for 1 minute on HIGH or until boiling and clear. Pour over the chops and vegetables and garnish with orange slices.

To serve 1 person, reduce the quantity of each ingredient by half, but cook for the same length of time.

warm vegetable salad instead of the red cabbage garnish.
To serve 1 person, prepare the complete recipe and use half. The other half will freeze well.

Spicy Steak Kebabs

PREPARATION TIME: 10 minutes, plus 1 hour to marinate meat

MICROWAVE COOKING TIME: 6 minutes

SERVES: 2 people

225g/8oz/½ lb sirloin steak, cut into 4cm
    (1½") cubes
1 leek, white part only
4 large mushrooms
4 cherry tomatoes
½ green pepper, sliced into 2.5cm
    (1") squares

MARINADE
30ml/1oz/2 tbsps oil
15ml/½ oz/1 tbsp lemon juice
½ clove garlic, crushed
1.25ml/¼ tsp ground cumin
1.25ml/¼ tsp ground coriander
1.25ml/¼ tsp gravy browning
Pinch Cayenne pepper
Salt and pepper

Mix the marinade ingredients together and put in the steak cubes, turning to coat evenly. Leave for 1 hour. Thread the meat and vegetables onto wooden skewers. Do not pack the ingredients too tightly together. Put on a roasting rack and cook on MEDIUM for about 6 minutes, turning and basting frequently until cooked as much as desired. Put remaining marinade into a smaller dish and cook for 2-3 minutes on HIGH until syrupy. Serve on a bed of rice. Pour the sauce over the cooked kebabs.
To serve one person, prepare only half of each ingredient, but cook for the same length of time.

Pheasant in Gin

PREPARATION TIME: 15 minutes

MICROWAVE COOKING TIME: 22 minutes

SERVES: 2 people

1 small pheasant, dressed (about
    675-790g/1½-1¾ lbs)
1 apple, peeled and chopped
60ml/2oz/¼ cup gin
5ml/1 tsp juniper berries
2.5ml/½ tsp rosemary
30ml/1oz/2 tbsps chicken bouillon
15g/½ oz/1 tbsp butter
7.5g/1½ tsps flour/plain flour
225g/8oz/1½ cups shredded red cabbage

Heat a browning dish for 5 minutes on HIGH. Put in the butter and, when foaming, add the pheasant. Cook for 3 minutes to lightly brown all sides of the pheasant, turning four times while cooking. Transfer to a medium-sized deep casserole and set aside. Add flour to the dish and scrape up any sediment. Cook for 1 minute to lightly brown the flour. De-glaze the pan with chicken bouillon and add the casserole with the remaining ingredients except the cabbage. Cover and cook for 10 minutes or until the pheasant is tender. It may be served slightly pink. During the last 3 minutes, add the red cabbage. Can be served with the

**This page: Spicy Steak Kebabs.
Facing page: Pheasant in Gin.**

Stuffed Chicken Breasts in Lemon Tarragon Cream

PREPARATION TIME: 15 minutes

MICROWAVE COOKING TIME: 18 minutes

SERVES: 2 people

2 boned chicken breast halves, skinned
5g/1 tsp butter
60g/2oz/½ cup finely chopped
  mushrooms
90g/3oz package/carton cream cheese
30ml/1oz/2 tbsps white wine
15ml/½ oz/1 tbsp lemon juice
Salt and pepper

SAUCE
15g/½ oz/1 tbsp butter
7.5g/½ tbsp flour/plain flour
Juice of ½ lemon
140ml/¼ pint/½ cup chicken stock
60ml/2oz/¼ cup heavy/double cream
2.5ml/½ tsp chopped tarragon, fresh or
  dried
Salt and pepper

GARNISH
Lemon slices

Cut a pocket along the thicker side of each chicken breast half. Melt 15g/1 tbsp butter for 30 seconds on HIGH in a small bowl. Add the white wine, salt and pepper, and mushrooms. Cook, uncovered, for 2 minutes on HIGH to soften the mushrooms. Cook for an additional 1 minute to evaporate liquid if excessive. Mix with the cream cheese and fill the pockets of the chicken. Put the breasts into a small casserole and sprinkle over the lemon juice and about 15ml/½ oz/1 tbsp water. Cover and cook for about 12 minutes on MEDIUM or until white and firm. Keep warm. In a small bowl melt 1 tbsp butter for 30 seconds on HIGH. Stir in the flour and add the stock and lemon juice gradually. Pour in any cooking liquid from the chicken and add the cream and tarragon. Cook for 1-2 minutes on HIGH, stirring every 30 seconds until thickened. Add salt and pepper. Spoon over the chicken breasts to serve and garnish with lemon slices. Serve with French peas or zucchini/courgette rolls.

To serve one person, reduce the quantity of each ingredient by half. Cook the mushroom filling for the same length of time, and the filled chicken breasts for 10 minutes on MEDIUM. Cook the sauce for about 1 minute on HIGH.

Chicken, Ham and Cheese Rolls with Mustard Sauce

PREPARATION TIME: 15 minutes

MICROWAVE COOKING TIME: 9 minutes

SERVES: 1 person

1 chicken breast half, skinned and boned
1 thin slice cooked ham
1 thin slice Swiss cheese
5ml/1 tsp chopped capers
5ml/1 tsp butter
30g/1oz/2½ tbsps cornflake crumbs
1.25ml/¼ tsp paprika
Salt and pepper

SAUCE
15g/½ oz/1 tbsp butter or margarine
15g/½ oz/1 tbsp flour/plain flour
140ml/¼ pint/½ cup milk
45ml/1½ oz/3 tbsps dry white wine
5ml/1 tsp Dijon mustard
5ml/1 tsp salad mustard
Salt and pepper

Place the chicken breast between 2 pieces of waxed/greaseproof paper and flatten with a meat mallet to about 3mm (⅛"). Lay the cheese on top of the slice of ham. Sprinkle on the capers, and roll up, folding in the sides, and fasten with wooden picks/cocktail sticks. Melt 5ml/1 tsp butter for 30 seconds on HIGH. Combine the cornflake crumbs with the paprika and salt and pepper on a sheet of waxed/greaseproof paper. Brush the chicken with the melted butter and then roll in the crumbs to coat. Push the crumb coating into the surface of the chicken. Put the chicken seam side down into a small casserole dish and cook, uncovered, on MEDIUM for 2 minutes. Turn over, cook for a further 1 minute on MEDIUM, and keep warm while

preparing the sauce. Melt 2.5ml/½ tbsp butter for 30 seconds on HIGH in a small bowl. Stir in the flour and add the milk and wine gradually. Stir in the mustards and salt and pepper. Cook, uncovered, for 1-2 minutes on HIGH, stirring every 30 seconds until thickened. Keep warm. Re-heat the chicken on HIGH for 2 minutes and serve with the sauce.

To serve 2 people, double all the ingredients. Cook the chicken for 4 minutes on MEDIUM and the sauce for 2-3 minutes on HIGH. Re-heat the chicken on HIGH for 2 minutes.

Rabbit with Olives

PREPARATION TIME: 15 minutes

MICROWAVE COOKING TIME: 23-28 minutes

SERVES: 2 people

2 rabbit pieces (hind- or fore-quarters)
30g/1oz/2 tbsps butter
10g/2 tsps flour/plain flour
1 shallot, chopped
60ml/2oz/¼ cup dry vermouth
60ml/2oz/¼ cup beef bouillon
60g/2oz/½ cup whole mushrooms
1.25ml/¼ tsp oregano
1.25ml/¼ tsp thyme
15ml/1 tbsp wholegrain mustard
12 stoned green olives, left whole
60ml/2oz/¼ cup heavy/double cream
Salt and pepper

Soak the rabbit overnight to whiten the meat, in enough water to cover, with a squeeze of lemon juice and a pinch of salt. Heat a browning dish for 5 minutes on HIGH. Melt the butter and cook the rabbit pieces for 2 minutes on HIGH, turning over after 1 minute to brown both sides. Remove from the dish to a 570ml/1 pint casserole. Add the mushrooms and shallot to the browning dish with the flour. Cook for 1 minute on HIGH to brown lightly. De-glaze the pan with the bouillon and pour the

Facing page: Chicken, Ham and Cheese Rolls with Mustard Sauce (top) and Stuffed Chicken Breasts in Lemon Tarragon Cream (bottom).

contents over the rabbit. Add the vermouth, herbs, mustard, and salt and pepper. Cover and cook on MEDIUM for 15-20 minutes, or until the rabbit is tender. After 10 minutes, add the olives and cream. Serve with rice or noodles.

To serve one person, half the complete recipe will freeze well.

Devilled Cornish Hen with Golden Rice Stuffing

PREPARATION TIME: 20 minutes

MICROWAVE COOKING TIME: 16 minutes

SERVES: 1 person

1 Cornish game hen/poussin (about 675g/1½ lbs)
30g/1oz/¼ cup quick-cooking rice
90ml/3oz/⅓ cup hot water
1 shallot, finely chopped
½ cap pimento, diced
15g/½ oz/1 tbsp chopped pecans
Pinch saffron
30ml/1oz/2 tbsps bottled steak sauce/ brown sauce
15g/½ oz/1 tbsp butter
2.5ml/½ tsp paprika
2.5ml/½ tsp dry mustard
2.5ml/½ tsp chili powder
5ml/1 tsp sugar
Pinch Cayenne pepper
60ml/2oz/¼ cup chicken bouillon
Salt and pepper

GARNISH
Small bunch watercress or parsley

Put the rice, saffron, shallot and hot water into a 570ml/1 pint casserole, cover, and cook on HIGH for 2 minutes or until the rice is tender and has absorbed all the color from the saffron. Add the pimento and pecans, and allow to cool slightly. Stuff the hen with rice. Mix together the spices, salt and pepper, and sugar. Melt 15g/½ oz/1 tbsp butter for 30 seconds on HIGH and brush it over the hen. Rub the spices over all surfaces of the hen. Close the cavity with wooden picks and place the hen, breast-side down, on a roasting rack. Combine remaining melted butter with the steak/brown sauce and any

remaining spices. Cook the hen for 5 minutes on HIGH and baste with the steak/brown sauce mixture. Turn breast-side up, cook for 5 minutes on HIGH, and baste. Cook for 2 minutes more, or until the juices run clear. Leave to stand for 5 minutes before serving. Add the chicken bouillon to the remaining sauce mixture, re-heat for 1-2 minutes on HIGH and pour over the hen to serve. Garnish with watercress or parsley.

To serve 2 people, double all quantities. Add 5 minutes to the cooking time for the hens.

This page: **Rabbit with Olives (top)** and **Venison Bourguignonne (bottom)**. Facing page: **Devilled Cornish Hen with Golden Rice Stuffing.**

Venison Bourguignonne

PREPARATION TIME: 15 minutes

MICROWAVE COOKING TIME: 36 minutes, plus 15 minutes standing time

SERVES: 2 people

225g/½ lb venison from the leg
1 thick-cut slice bacon, cut into 5mm (¼")
    pieces
60g/2oz/½ cup small onions
30g/1oz/¼ cup mushrooms, quartered
½ clove garlic, crushed
15g/½ oz/1 tbsp butter
15g/½ oz/1 tbsp flour/plain flour
90ml/3oz/⅓ cup red wine
200ml/6oz/¾ cup beef bouillon
5ml/1 tsp tomato paste
1 bay leaf
5ml/¼ tsp thyme
Salt and pepper

Melt the butter for 30 seconds on
HIGH in a large casserole. Add the
onion, bacon, mushrooms and garlic,
and cook for 1 minute on HIGH until
slightly brown. Remove from the
casserole and set aside. Add the
venison and cook for 2-3 minutes on
HIGH, stirring occasionally to brown
slightly. Sprinkle on the flour, and
cook for a further minute on HIGH.
Stir in the wine, bouillon and tomato
paste. Add the thyme and bay leaf
and cover the casserole. Cook,
stirring occasionally, for 15 minutes
on MEDIUM. Add the remaining
ingredients, re-cover the casserole,
and cook for another 15 minutes
on MEDIUM. Leave to stand for
15 minutes before serving. Serve
with boiled potatoes or noodles.
To serve one person, cook the full
recipe, use half and the other half will
freeze well.

Fiery Duck

PREPARATION TIME: 15-20 minutes,
plus 30-60 minutes to marinate duck

MICROWAVE COOKING TIME:
8 minutes, plus 1 minute standing time

SERVES: 2 people

½ a duck breast, boned and skinned –
    about 225g/½ lb. If duck parts are
    unavailable, cut a whole duck into
    quarters and freeze the leg portions.
½ a small red pepper, sliced into 5mm
    (¼") strips
2 sticks celery, thinly sliced
120g/4oz/1 cup beansprouts
2 green/spring onions, sliced
60g/2oz/½ cup roasted cashew nuts

2.5-5ml/½-1 tsp Szechuan pepper, or
    crushed dried chili peppers
2.5ml/½ tsp cornstarch/cornflour
60ml/2oz/¼ cup chicken bouillon

MARINADE
10ml/2 tsps rice or cider vinegar
10ml/2 tsps soy sauce
10ml/2 tsps sherry
10ml/2 tsps sesame seed oil
Pinch ground ginger
½ clove crushed garlic
Salt and pepper

Remove the skin and bone from the
breast portions and cut the duck into
thin strips. Combine the marinade
ingredients in a medium-sized bowl
and stir in the duck pieces. Cover the
bowl and chill for 30-60 minutes.
Drain the duck, reserving the
marinade, and mix the cornstarch/
cornflour, bouillon and Szechuan or
chili pepper with the marinade. Put
the duck into a large casserole and
pour over sauce. Stir to mix, cover
the dish and cook for 10 minutes on
MEDIUM, stirring occasionally. Add
the red pepper and celery to the
casserole and cook for a further
2 minutes on HIGH. Stir in the
cashews, onions and beansprouts.
Serve with fried rice or crisp noodles.
Best prepared for 2 people.

Turkey Korma (Mild Curry)

PREPARATION TIME: 15 minutes

MICROWAVE COOKING TIME:
10 minutes

SERVES: 1 person

1 turkey leg
30g/1oz/2 tbsps chopped onion
5ml/1 tsp oil
7.5g/1½ tsps butter or margarine
7.5ml/½ tbsp curry powder
5ml/1 tsp paprika
5ml/1 tsp ground coriander
25g/¾ oz/1½ tbsps flour/plain flour
140ml/¼ pint/½ cup chicken bouillon
15g/½ oz/1 tbsp golden raisins
15g/½ oz/1 tbsp roasted cashew nuts or
    shelled pistachio nuts
10ml/2 tsps unsweetened coconut

60ml/2oz/¼ cup plain yogurt
Salt and pepper

Skin and bone the turkey leg and cut
the meat into 2.5cm (1") pieces. Use
half and freeze the other half for use
later. Heat the oil in a large casserole
for 30 seconds on HIGH. Add the
butter and, when melted, add the
onion, turkey and spices. Cook for 3
minutes on HIGH to cook the spices.
Add the flour and bouillon and stir
to mix well. Cover the casserole and
cook for 5 minutes on HIGH, stirring
frequently until the turkey is tender.
Add the raisins, coconut, nuts, salt,
pepper and yogurt. Leave to stand,
covered, for 1 minute. Serve with rice
and chutney.
To serve 2 people, use the whole
turkey leg and double all other
ingredients. Cook the casserole for 8
minutes on HIGH.

Ham Steaks with Mango Sauce

PREPARATION TIME: 10 minutes

MICROWAVE COOKING TIME:
13 minutes

SERVES: 2 people

2 fully cooked ham slices (about 120g/
    ¼ lb each)
15g/½ oz/1 tbsp butter

SAUCE
1 ripe mango, peeled and thinly sliced
2.5ml/½ tsp ground ginger
Juice of half a lime
2.5ml/½ tsp soy sauce
Pinch Cayenne pepper
1.25ml/¼ tsp cornstarch/cornflour
90ml/3oz/⅓ cup orange juice

Cut the ham slices around the
outside at 5cm (2") intervals, 5mm
(¼") in from the edge, to stop them
from curling. Reserve 4 thin slices of
mango and purée the rest in a food
processor with the remaining sauce
ingredients. Heat a browning dish on

Facing page: Fiery Duck (top) and
Turkey Korma (Mild Curry)
(bottom).

HIGH for 5 minutes. Put in the butter and the ham steaks and cook for 1 minute on HIGH. Turn the ham steaks once to brown both sides. Remove the ham from the dish to a casserole and pour over the puréed sauce ingredients. Cook, uncovered, for about 5 minutes on MEDIUM, or until the sauce has thickened. If necessary, remove the ham and keep warm while cooking the sauce for a further 2 minutes on HIGH. Garnish with the reserved mango slices. Serve with sesame stir-fry.

To serve one person, use 1 ham slice and 7.5g/½ tbsp butter. Use full quantity sauce ingredients and cook for the same length of time as for 2 people.

Beef Roulades

PREPARATION TIME: 20 minutes

MICROWAVE COOKING TIME: 19 minutes

SERVES: 2 people

4 pieces rump steak, cut thin and
*   flattened*
1 dill pickle, cut into quarters lengthwise
2 green/spring onions, trimmed and cut
*   in half lengthwise*
15ml/1 tbsp oil

SAUCE
60g/2oz/½ cup mushrooms, quartered
7.5g/1½ tsp butter or margarine
10ml/2 tsps flour
1.25ml/¼ tsp thyme
1 bay leaf
180ml/5oz/⅔ cup beef bouillon
15ml/½ oz/1 tbsp red wine
Salt and pepper
Gravy browning (if necessary)

GARNISH
Buttered spinach pasta

Roll each of the beef slices around a quarter of the dill pickle and half a green/spring onion. Sprinkle with pepper and fasten with wooden picks/cocktail sticks. Heat a browning dish on HIGH for 5 minutes. Put in the oil and add the roulades. Cook for 8 minutes, turning frequently. Remove from the dish and set aside in a casserole dish.

Add the butter to the dish and allow to melt. Add the mushrooms and cook for 1 minute on HIGH. Stir in the flour and cook for 2 minutes to brown lightly. Add the bouillon, wine, thyme and bay leaf, scraping any sediment off the surface of the browning dish. Add gravy browning for extra color if necessary. Season, and pour over the roulades. Cover the dish and cook for 12 minutes on MEDIUM. Test the meat with a knife and if not tender, cook for a further 3 minutes on HIGH. Serve with the pasta or French peas.

To serve one person, prepare only half the quantity of each ingredient and cook the roulades in the sauce for about 10 minutes on MEDIUM. Alternatively, the full quantity recipe freezes well.

Mexican Pork Casserole

PREPARATION TIME: 15 minutes

MICROWAVE COOKING TIME: 28 minutes

SERVES: 2 people

225g/8oz/½ lb boneless pork loin, cut
*   into 2.5cm (1″) cubes*

peppers, cover, and cook on
MEDIUM for 17 minutes, or until
the pork loses its pink color. Add the
beans and heat for 2 minutes on
MEDIUM. Serve with tortilla chips if
desired.
To serve 1 person, prepare full
quantity casserole, and freeze half.

Veal Chops in Peppercorn Cream Sauce

PREPARATION TIME: 15 minutes

MICROWAVE COOKING TIME:
25 minutes

SERVES: 2 people

2 loin veal chops
15g/½ oz/1 tbsp butter or margarine
140ml/¼ pint/½ cup heavy/ double
    cream
60ml/2oz/¼ cup chicken bouillon
30ml/½ oz/2 tbsps brandy
15ml/1 tbsp green peppercorns, dried (or
    packed in brine, drained and rinsed)
½ cap pimento, diced
2 black olives, stoned and sliced thinly
Salt and pepper

Remove some of the fat from the
outside of the chops. Heat a
browning dish on HIGH for
5 minutes. Put in the butter or
margarine and the chops. Cook for
3 minutes on HIGH, turning once,
until both sides are lightly browned.
Remove the chops to a casserole. De-
glaze the dish with the bouillon and
add the brandy, salt and pepper. Pour
the sauce over the chops, cover with
pierced plastic wrap, and cook on
MEDIUM for 15 minutes or until the
chops are tender. Add the
peppercorns, pimento and olives
during the last 3 minutes of cooking
time. If the chops are not tender after
15 minutes, cook for an additional
2 minutes on MEDIUM. Add the
cream and cook 1 minute on HIGH.
Serve with zucchini/courgette rolls,
leeks Provençale, or French peas.
To serve 1 person, cut the quantities
of each ingredient by half and cook
for the same length of time.

90g/3oz/½ cup canned garbanzo beans/
    chickpeas
90g/3oz/½ cup canned kidney beans
30g/1oz/¼ cup chopped sweet red pepper
30g/1oz/¼ cup chopped green pepper
½ small chili pepper, finely chopped
30g/1oz/¼ cup chopped onion
15g/½ oz/1 tbsp flour/plain flour
10ml/2 tsps oil
200ml/6oz/¾ cup beef bouillon/stock
15ml/1 tbsp instant coffee
½ clove garlic, crushed
1.25ml/¼ tsp ground cumin
1.25ml/¼ tsp ground coriander

GARNISH
Tortilla chips

**Facing page: Veal Chops in
Peppercorn Cream Sauce (top)
and Ham Steaks with Mango
Sauce (bottom). This page:
Mexican Pork Casserole (top) and
Beef Roulades (bottom).**

Heat a browning dish for 5 minutes
on HIGH. Put in the oil and add the
pork cubes. Cook for 2 minutes on
HIGH, stirring frequently, until
slightly browned. Add the cumin,
coriander, garlic, onion and flour, and
cook for 1-2 minutes on HIGH.
Dissolve the instant coffee in the
bouillon/stock and add to the
casserole, stirring well. Add the

VEGETABLES

Corn on the Cob with Flavored Butters

PREPARATION TIME: 10 minutes

MICROWAVE COOKING TIME: 8 minutes

SERVES: 2 people

2 ears of corn
45g/1½ oz/3 tbsps butter with a choice
    of:
2.5ml/½ tsp wholegrain mustard, or
2.5ml/½ tsp tomato purée and
    1.25ml/¼ tsp basil, or
2.5ml/½ tsp garlic powder and
    1.25ml/¼ tsp parsley, or
2.5ml/½ tsp chili powder

Clean the husks and silk from the ears/cobs of corn and wrap each in plastic wrap, or put into a roasting bag and seal tightly. Cook for about 8 minutes, turning once. Mix the butter with one or more of the flavoring choices and serve with the hot corn.

Leeks Provençale

PREPARATION TIME: 10 minutes

MICROWAVE COOKING TIME: 8 minutes

SERVES: 2 people

3 leeks, washed, trimmed and cut into
    5cm (2") pieces
1 small clove garlic, finely chopped
2 tomatoes, chopped
15ml/1 tbsp oil
30ml/2 tbsps white wine
2.5ml/½ tsp thyme
15ml/1 tbsp chopped parsley
Salt and pepper

Put the oil into a 1150ml/2 pint/ 1 quart casserole, and add the leeks and garlic, tossing to coat. Cook, uncovered, for 3 minutes on HIGH, stirring occasionally. Add the herbs,

This page: Corn on the Cob with Flavored Butters. Facing page: French Peas (top) and Leeks Provençale (bottom).

white wine, salt and pepper, and cover and cook for a further 5 minutes on HIGH. Add the tomatoes and cook for 1 minute on HIGH. Serve immediately.
To serve one person, use 1 large or 2 small leeks and half of each of the other ingredients. Cook the leeks for 2 minutes on HIGH and after adding the other ingredients, cook for a further 3-4 minutes on HIGH. Add the tomatoes and cook for 1 minute on HIGH.

Eggplant/Aubergine Niramish

PREPARATION TIME: 20 minutes

MICROWAVE COOKING TIME: 17 minutes

SERVES: 2 people

1 eggplant/aubergine
30g/1oz/2 tbsps butter
1 clove garlic, finely chopped
1 small onion, chopped
1 small potato, diced
1 small carrot, diced
30g/1oz/¼ cup peas
225g/8oz/1 cup canned tomatoes, chopped and juice reserved
5ml/1 tsp flour/plain flour
30g/1oz/¼ cup raisins
30g/1oz/¼ cup pine nuts or chopped almonds
15ml/1 tbsp chopped coriander leaves or parsley
1.25ml/¼ tsp ground coriander
1.25ml/¼ tsp ground cumin
1.25ml/¼ tsp turmeric
1.25ml/¼ tsp fenugreek
1.25ml/¼ tsp ground ginger
Cayenne pepper
Paprika
Salt and pepper

GARNISH
60ml/2oz/¼ cup plain yogurt
Parsley or coriander leaves

Cut the eggplant/aubergine in half lengthwise and score the flesh lightly. Sprinkle with salt and leave to stand for 20 minutes. The salt will draw out any bitterness. Rinse the eggplant well and pat dry. Melt the butter for 30 seconds on HIGH in a large

casserole. Add the spices and cook for 2 minutes on HIGH. Add the onion, garlic, carrots and potatoes. Cover and cook for 3 minutes on HIGH. Stir in the flour and add the tomato juice and pulp and chopped coriander or parsley. Cover the bowl and cook on HIGH for a further 5 minutes or until vegetables are just tender. Add the raisins, nuts and peas. Put the eggplant in another casserole, cover, and cook for 5 minutes on HIGH. Scoop out the flesh and reserve the skins. Mix the eggplant with the vegetable filling and fill the skins. Sprinkle with paprika and cook for 3 minutes on HIGH. Serve immediately. Top with a spoonful of yogurt and garnish with sprigs of parsley or coriander.
To serve 1 person, prepare the full quantity, serve one half and freeze the other.

French Peas

PREPARATION TIME: 10 minutes

MICROWAVE COOKING TIME: 6-10 minutes

SERVES: 2 people

225g/8oz/1½ cups peas, fresh or frozen
4 leaves Romaine/cos lettuce
60g/2oz/½ cup parsley or chervil sprigs
120g/4oz/½ cup small onions, peeled
5ml/1 tsp sugar
15g/½ oz/1 tbsp butter
15g/½ oz/1 tbsp flour/plain flour
2 sticks celery, diced
140ml/¼ pint/½ cup chicken bouillon/stock
Salt and pepper

If using fresh peas, shell them and combine with the celery, onions, half the bouillon/stock, salt and pepper, and sugar in a 1150ml/2 pint/1 quart casserole. Cover and cook for 7 minutes on HIGH until almost tender. Add the lettuce and parsley (or chervil) and cook for a further 2 minutes on HIGH. Set aside. (If using frozen peas, combine the lettuce and parsley at the beginning and cook for a total of 5 minutes.) Melt the butter in a small bowl for 30 seconds on HIGH. Add the flour and remaining stock, and cook,

uncovered, for 1 minute on HIGH. Stir into the peas, and serve. Best cooked for 2 people.

Stuffed Potatoes

PREPARATION TIME: 15 minutes

MICROWAVE COOKING TIME: 18 minutes, plus 5 minutes standing time

SERVES: 1 person

1 large baking potato
10ml/2 tsps chopped chives
30ml/1oz/2 tbsps milk
2 strips bacon
30ml/1oz/2 tbsps sour cream
15g/½ oz/1 tbsp crumbled blue cheese
15g/½ oz/1 tbsp shredded/grated Cheddar cheese
15ml/1 tbsp dry seasoned breadcrumbs
Paprika
Salt and pepper

Heat a browning dish for 5 minutes on HIGH. Put in the bacon and cook for 2-3 minutes on HIGH, or until crisp. Crumble the bacon and set it aside. Pierce the potato skin several times with a fork. Put the potato on a plate and cook on HIGH for 5 minutes, or until soft. Turn over after 2 minutes. Cover it tightly in foil and leave it to stand for 5 minutes. Cut the potato in half lengthwise and scoop out the flesh, reserving the shells. Heat the milk for 30 seconds on HIGH, add to the potato with the sour cream and beat well. Add the chives, salt and pepper, bacon and blue cheese, and spoon into the potato shells. Sprinkle on the Cheddar cheese, crumbs and paprika. Cook on MEDIUM for 3 minutes and increase the setting to HIGH for 1 minute. Serve immediately.
For two people, use the full quantity recipe for a side dish, or double the quantity of each ingredient. Cook the potatoes for 7 minutes on HIGH, and the filled potato shells for 4 minutes on MEDIUM and 1 minute on HIGH.

Facing page: Eggplant/Aubergine Niramish (top) and Stuffed Potatoes (bottom).

Zucchini/Courgette Rolls

PREPARATION TIME: 15 minutes

MICROWAVE COOKING TIME:
8 minutes

SERVES: 2 people

1 large zucchini/courgette
1 carrot, cut into 8cm (3") sticks
1 green pepper, cut into 12mm (½") slices
2 green/spring onions, shredded
  lengthwise
Small bunch of whole fresh chives
1.25ml/¼ tsp herbs (thyme or basil)
15g/½ oz/1 tbsp butter
Juice of half a lemon
Salt and pepper

Trim the end of the zucchini/
courgette and cut lengthwise into
very thin slices. Spread evenly over
the bottom of a large casserole. Pour
on the lemon juice, cover, and cook
for 1 minute to soften. Remove and
set aside. In the same casserole, cook
the carrot, covered, for 3 minutes on
HIGH. Add the pepper and cook for
a further 2 minutes on HIGH. Add
the onion. Sprinkle with herbs and
salt and pepper. Divide the
vegetables evenly and place on top of
the zucchini/courgette slices, twisting
the ends of the zucchini around the
piles of vegetables. Tie at both ends
with the chives. Melt the butter in a
small bowl for 30 seconds on HIGH.
Pour the butter over the vegetables in
the casserole, cover, and heat
through for 1-2 minutes on HIGH
before serving. Best cooked for 2
people.

Sesame Stir-fry

PREPARATION TIME: 15 minutes

MICROWAVE COOKING TIME:
7 minutes

SERVES: 2 people

30ml/2 tbsps oil
60g/2oz/¼ lb pea pods/mangetout
1 stick celery, sliced
2 ears baby corn, cut in half lengthwise
60g/2oz/¼ cup water chestnuts, sliced
30g/1oz/¼ cup mushrooms, sliced
120g/4oz/1 cup beansprouts
1 green/spring onion, diagonally sliced

120g/4oz/1 cup Chinese cabbage,
  shredded
2.5ml/½ tsp chopped ginger root
1 small sweet red pepper, thinly sliced
15g/½ oz/1 tbsp cornstarch/cornflour
30ml/2 tbsps soy sauce
15ml/1 tbsp sherry
2.5ml/½ tsp sesame seed oil
15g/½ oz/1 tbsp sesame seeds
60ml/2oz/¼ cup water

Heat a browning tray for 5 minutes
on HIGH. Put in 30ml/2 tbsps of oil
and add all the vegetables except the
Chinese cabbage and green onion.
Toss in the oil and add the ginger and
sesame seeds. Cook on HIGH for
4 minutes. Add the Chinese cabbage
and beansprouts and cook for
1 minute more on HIGH. Combine

**This page: Zucchini/Courgette
Rolls.
Facing page: Sesame Stir-fry.**

the cornstarch, sherry, soy sauce,
water and sesame seed oil in a small
bowl. Cook on HIGH for 2 minutes,
or until clear. Pour over the vegetables and toss to coat before serving.
To serve one person, cut the ingredient quantities by half and cook the
vegetables for 3 minutes on HIGH.
Add the cabbage and beansprouts
and cook for 30 seconds on HIGH.
Cook the sauce ingredients for
2 minutes on HIGH.

Warm Vegetable Salad

PREPARATION TIME: 20 minutes

MICROWAVE COOKING TIME:
5 minutes

SERVES: 2 people

60g/2oz/¼ cup shredded red cabbage
60g/2oz/¼ cup green beans
30g/1oz/¼ cup sliced mushrooms
4 green/spring onions, trimmed
1 hard-boiled egg
Shredded lettuce

DRESSING
25ml/1½ tbsps oil
15ml/1 tbsp vinegar
15ml/1 tbsp Dijon mustard
2.5ml/½ tsp caraway seeds
Salt and pepper

Mix the dressing ingredients together
thoroughly. Chop the white of the egg
and push the yolk through a strainer.
Put the cabbage, beans, onions and
mushrooms into a 570ml/1 pint
casserole with 15ml/1 tbsp water and
cook, covered, for 5 minutes. Add
the lettuce and dressing during the
last minute of cooking, and toss well.
Serve garnished with the egg.
For one person, reduce the ingredient
quantities by half, except for the egg.
Cook the vegetables for 3-4 minutes
before adding the lettuce and
dressing.

Lima Beans, Carrots and Bacon with Mustard

PREPARATION TIME: 15 minutes

MICROWAVE COOKING TIME:
11 minutes

SERVES: 2 people

120g/4oz/1 cup Lima beans
120g/4oz/1 cup sliced carrots
2 strips bacon
15ml/1 tbsp Dijon mustard
25g/¾ oz/1½ tbsps butter
Salt and pepper

Heat a browning dish for 5 minutes
on HIGH. Cook the bacon for
1-2 minutes on HIGH or until crisp.
Crumble the bacon and set it aside.

Put the beans into a 570ml/1 pint
casserole with 30ml/1oz/2 tbsps
water and cook for 1 minute on
HIGH. Peel off the outer skin if
desired and set the beans aside. Put
the carrots into the casserole with
2 tbsps water. Cook, uncovered, for
2 minutes on HIGH. Add the peeled
beans to the casserole and cook for
1 minute more on HIGH. Drain and
keep warm. Add the bacon to the
beans and carrots. In a small bowl,
melt the butter for 30 seconds on

**This page: Warm Vegetable Salad
(top) and Lima Beans, Carrots and
Bacon with Mustard (bottom).
Facing page: Raspberry
Meringues.**

HIGH. Add the salt and pepper, and
beat in the mustard until the sauce
holds together. Pour over the vegetables and toss to serve.
For one person, cut the quantity of
each ingredient by half and cook for
half the stated time.

DESSERTS

Raspberry Meringues

PREPARATION TIME: 15 minutes

MICROWAVE COOKING TIME:
1 minutes

SERVES: 2 people

MERINGUES
1 egg white
120g/4oz/1 cup powdered/icing sugar
2.5ml/½ tsp raspberry flavoring
2 drops red food coloring

FILLING
140ml/¼ pint/½ cup cream, whipped
120g/4oz/1 cup fresh or frozen
  raspberries
30ml/½ oz/2 tbsps raspberry liqueur
Sugar

GARNISH
Powdered/icing sugar
Cocoa

Put the egg white into a bowl and stir with a fork. Stir in the powdered/icing sugar, adding enough to make a firm, pliable dough. Add the coloring and flavoring with the powdered/icing sugar. Roll to 1.5cm (½") thick on a board sprinkled with powdered/icing sugar. Cut into 5cm (2") heart shapes or rounds and place 10cm (4") apart on a microwave baking sheet lined with wax/greaseproof paper. If making heart shapes, have the points towards the middle. Cook for 1 minute on HIGH until firm and dry. Combine the raspberries, liqueur and sugar to taste. When the meringues are cool, fill with some of the raspberries and sandwich 2 of the meringues together with cream. Sprinkle the tops with powdered/icing sugar and cocoa. Serve remaining raspberries separately.

thickened. Stir in the kirsch. Serve the pudding warm with the sauce, and whipped cream or ice cream if desired.

Oranges in Caramel Sauce

PREPARATION TIME: 15 minutes

MICROWAVE COOKING TIME: 4 minutes

SERVES: 1 person

1 orange
45g/1½ oz/3 tbsps brown sugar
60ml/2oz/¼ cup water
5ml/1 tsp Grand Marnier
2.5ml/½ tsp cornstarch/cornflour
1.25ml/¼ tsp lemon juice

Peel the orange, removing all the white pith. Set aside the whole orange and scrape all the pith off the peel. Cut the orange peel into thin strips. Mix the brown sugar, water and lemon juice and heat for 2 minutes on HIGH. Stir occasionally to help dissolve the sugar. Mix the cornstarch/cornflour and the liqueur and stir into the sugar syrup. Cook for 1 minute on HIGH to thicken. Add the orange peel to the hot sauce and pour over the orange. Heat through for 1 minute on HIGH, turning once. Serve immediately.

Cherry and Almond Bread Pudding

PREPARATION TIME: 15 minutes

MICROWAVE COOKING TIME: 9-14 minutes

SERVES: 2 people

60g/2oz/¼ cup chopped, unblanched almonds
1 egg
200ml/6oz/¾ cup light cream
90g/3oz/1½ cups brioche, cut into 5cm (2") cubes
1.25ml/¼ tsp cinnamon
45g/1½ oz/3 tbsps sugar
90g/3oz/½ cup pitted dark, sweet cherries, canned, and juice reserved

SAUCE
140ml/¼ pint/½ cup reserved cherry juice
1.25ml/¼ tsp cornstarch/cornflour
15ml/1 tbsp cherry brandy or kirsch
1.25ml/¼ tsp almond extract/essence

Heat a browning dish for 5 minutes on HIGH. Put in the almonds and cook on HIGH for about 3 minutes, stirring every 30 seconds until golden brown. Combine the egg and cream. Beat in the sugar and cinnamon, and stir in the bread cubes and cherries. Pour into a 570ml/1 pint casserole and cook for 5-10 minutes on HIGH, or until the center is just set. Leave to stand for 2 minutes before serving. Combine the juice, extract and cornstarch. Cook on HIGH for 1 minute, stirring once or twice until

Cranberry Crisp

PREPARATION TIME: 10 minutes

MICROWAVE COOKING TIME: 11-12 minutes

SERVES: 2 people

FILLING
140ml/¼ pint/½ cup orange juice or cranberry juice
120g/4oz/1 cup fresh cranberries
10ml/2 tsps sugar
10ml/2 tsps cornstarch/cornflour
1.25ml/¼ tsp cinnamon

This page: Oranges in Caramel Sauce. Facing page: Cherry and Almond Bread Pudding (top) and Cranberry Crisp (bottom).

TOPPING
225g/8oz/¾ cup crunchy oatmeal cereal
30g/1oz/2 tbsps butter or margarine
15g/½ oz/1 tbsp flour/plain flour
30ml/1oz/2 tbsps honey

Combine the filling ingredients in a small casserole or individual dishes and cook on HIGH for 3-4 minutes, or until the mixture thickens. Stir twice during cooking and set aside. Toss the flour and cereal together. Melt the butter and mix in. Sprinkle over the top of the cranberry filling and cook for 4 minutes on HIGH. Drizzle over the honey and cook for a further 4 minutes on HIGH. Serve warm, with whipped cream.

Black Velvet and White Lace

PREPARATION TIME: 25 minutes

MICROWAVE COOKING TIME: 5 minutes

SERVES: 2 people

BLACK VELVET
120g/4oz/½ cup unsalted butter
60g/2oz/¼ cup sugar
2 eggs, separated
120g/4oz/4 squares cooking chocolate
15g/½ oz/1 tbsp instant coffee dissolved in 30ml/1oz/2 tbsps boiling water

WHITE LACE
120g/¼ lb white chocolate

Soften the butter in a medium-sized bowl for 20 seconds on HIGH. Add sugar and beat until light and fluffy. Add the egg yolks one at a time, beating between each addition until the mixture is light and lemon-colored. Melt the chocolate with the strong coffee mixture for 2 minutes on MEDIUM. Whisk the egg whites until stiff but not dry. Beat the warm chocolate into the egg yolks quickly and heat 2 minutes on MEDIUM, stirring every 30 seconds. Fold in the egg whites. Refrigerate until firm. Put the white chocolate into a small bowl and melt on MEDIUM for 1-2 minutes, stirring once. Fill a small pastry piping bag fitted with a writing tube/nozzle. Pipe out a lacy pattern

onto wax/bakewell paper and refrigerate to harden. To serve, scoop out spoonfuls of the mousse into bowls or onto plates. Pour over 15ml/1 tbsp of coffee liqueur if desired. Carefully peel off the white chocolate lace patterns and use to decorate the black velvet mousse.

Brown Sugar Bananas

PREPARATION TIME: 10 minutes

MICROWAVE COOKING TIME: 3½ minutes

SERVES: 2 people

2 bananas
30g/1oz/2 tbsps butter or margarine
60g/2oz/4 tbsps brown sugar
Grated rind and juice of 1 lemon
60g/2oz/¼ cup whole pecans
30ml/1oz/2 tbsps dark rum

Peel the bananas and cut in half lengthwise. Brush all surfaces with lemon juice to prevent browning. Melt the butter in a baking dish for 30 seconds on HIGH. Add the lemon juice and rind. Add the bananas and cook on MEDIUM for 2 minutes until heated through. Remove the bananas and keep them warm. Stir in the sugar and cook for 1 minute on HIGH, stirring frequently until bubbling. Add the pecans and rum, and pour over the bananas to serve.

Orange Creams

PREPARATION TIME: 15-20 minutes

MICROWAVE COOKING TIME: 5 minutes

SERVES: 2 people

30ml/1oz/2 tbsps orange juice
200ml/6oz/¾ cup milk
2 eggs, beaten
60g/2oz/¼ cup sugar
Ground ginger
1 tangerine
1 egg white
Granulated sugar

Peel the tangerine, removing all the white pith. Leave the membranes around each segment. Beat the egg white lightly and dip in the segments. Roll in the granulated sugar and put on wax/greaseproof paper to set. Heat the milk on HIGH for 2 minutes in a 570ml/1 pint/2 cup measure: do not allow the milk to boil. Add the orange juice. Mix the eggs, sugar, ginger and a pinch of salt. Beat well and gradually add the milk. Pour into 2 custard cups/ramekin dishes, and put them into a baking dish with hot water to come 5mm (¼″) up the outsides of the cups/dishes. Cover the baking dish loosely with plastic wrap and cook for 3 minutes on LOW. If softly set, remove from the oven and allow to cool. If still liquid, cook for 1½ minutes more on LOW, watching carefully. Serve warm or cold with the frosted tangerines.

Grenadine and Lemon Pears

PREPARATION TIME: 15 minutes

MICROWAVE COOKING TIME: 15-20 minutes

SERVES: 2 people

2 fresh pears, approximately equal size
Juice and peel of 1 lemon
280ml/½ pint/1 cup Grenadine syrup
140ml/¼ pint/½ cup light corn syrup
60ml/2oz/¼ cup water

GARNISH
Mint leaves

Mix the corn syrup, water and Grenadine syrup and cook for 5 minutes on HIGH. Peel the lemon and cut the peel into very thin strips. Squeeze the juice from the lemon and mix with the syrup. Peel the pears and leave whole. Leave the stem attached, but remove the eye on

Facing page: Orange Creams (top) and Brown Sugar Bananas (bottom).

the base. Put the pears into a small, deep bowl, big enough for them to stand upright in. Pour over the syrup and cover the bowl with pierced plastic wrap. Cook for 5 minutes on HIGH. Lower the setting to MEDIUM and cook 5 minutes, or until tender. If not tender after 5

minutes, cook for a further 5 minutes on MEDIUM. Remove the pears from the syrup and re-boil the syrup for 5 minutes on HIGH to reduce. Stir in the peel and coat over the pears. Garnish with the mint leaves, and serve hot or cold with whipped cream.

This page: Black Velvet and White Lace. Facing page: Grenadine and Lemon Pears.

INDEX